14.50

D0948687

ARISTOTLE'S CONCEPT OF DIALECTIC

ARISTOTLE'S CONCEPT OF DIALECTIC

J. D. G. EVANS

FELLOW OF SIDNEY SUSSEX COLLEGE, CAMBRIDGE

CAMBRIDGE UNIVERSITY PRESS

CAMBRIDGE

LONDON · NEW YORK · MELBOURNE

Published by the Syndics of the Cambridge University Press
The Pitt Building, Trumpington Street, Cambridge CB2 1RP
Bentley House, 200 Euston Road, London NW1 2DB
32 East 57th Street, New York, NY 10022, USA
296 Beaconsfield Parade, Middle Park, Melbourne 3206, Australia

© Cambridge University Press 1977

First published 1977

Printed in Great Britain by
Western Printing Services Ltd
Bristol

Library of Congress Cataloguing in Publication Data

Evans, John David Gemmill, 1942–
    Aristotle's concept of dialectic.

    Bibliography: p.
    Includes indexes.
        1.   Aristoteles – Logic.   I.   Title.
B491.L8E9   185   76–22982
ISBN 0 521 21425 4

TO MY MOTHER AND FATHER

TEXTS AND ABBREVIATIONS

In all cases where there are Oxford Classical Texts of the works of Plato and Aristotle I have used them. For the *De Partibus Animalium* and the *Eudemian Ethics* I have used the Loeb editions of A. L. Peck and H. Rackham respectively. The fragments of Aristotle's works are cited under the numeration of Ross (*Aristotelis Fragmenta Selecta*, Oxford 1955); but for ease of reference I have generally added the *testimonia* for fragments quoted.

I have referred to the works of Plato and Aristotle by the following abbreviations:

Plato	*Crat.*	*Cratylus*
	Parm.	*Parmenides*
	Phaedr.	*Phaedrus*
	Phil.	*Philebus*
	Pol.	*Politicus*
	Rep.	*Republic*
	Soph.	*Sophist*
	Symp.	*Symposium*
	Theaet.	*Theaetetus*
Aristotle	*Cat.*	*Categories*
	De Int.	*De Interpretatione*
	An. Pr.	*Prior Analytics*
	An. Post.	*Posterior Analytics*
	Top.	*Topics*
	SE	*Sophistici Elenchi*
	Phys.	*Physics*
	De An.	*De Anima*
	PA	*De Partibus Animalium*
	Met.	*Metaphysics*
	EN	*Nicomachean Ethics*
	EE	*Eudemian Ethics*
	Pol.	*Politics*
	Rhet.	*Rhetoric*

CONTENTS

CONTENTS

PREFACE

The notion of dialectic is a piece of intellectual currency which, like the currency of cash, is more used than understood. Most of those who use it are aware of it only in its more recent cultural forms and are unfamiliar with its historical genesis among the philosophers of ancient Greece. So although this book is a reworking of a dissertation which was approved for the Cambridge PhD degree, and engages in the range of scholarly debate which surrounds the issues under discussion, I hope that it may reach a wider audience than those who professionally rejoice under the title of ancient philosopher.

To this end all quotations from the Greek have been translated and all the key terms are transliterated; I append a glossary to assist understanding of this aspect of the book. Fairness to the reader and scholarly accuracy alike require that this should produce what is in some places a spiny text. To attempt to smooth the rough edges would have the effect of begging questions of interpretation, as has happened too often with material of this sort.

My many debts to others are acknowledged in the text and the bibliography. The dissertation was examined by Professor W. K. C. Guthrie and Professor A. C. Lloyd, and I am grateful to them for numerous helpful comments. My greatest debt is to Professor G. E. L. Owen and Mr Renford Bambrough who have commented on this work at various stages in its preparation. Both have greatly aided my understanding of Aristotle by their writings and their oral instruction; and I count it a privilege to have been able to learn from these great Aristotelian exegetes. My interest in dialectic and the *Topics* was first aroused by Owen. His work has continued to suggest many lines of approach and to draw my attention to many texts which have been useful in this study; and it has always served as a model of Aristotelian interpretation. I owe to Bambrough an appreciation of the help which the philosophical insights of Wittgenstein and Wisdom can provide for the interpreter of Plato and Aristotle. In his work he has performed the great service of indicating the continuity between the concerns of these modern thinkers and the philosophical tradition which they themselves do little explicitly to recognise.

PREFACE

I acknowledge with gratitude the decision of the Syndics of the Cambridge University Press to undertake the publication of this book and the unfailing help of their staff in producing it. I wish particularly to thank Dr Jeremy Mynott for the sympathetic tact which he has shown in prodding an unpunctual author, as well as for useful advice on a number of points.

I dedicate this book to my mother and father, the ultimate causes of its matter and form.

I

INTRODUCTION

Historical background

Aristotle's official presentation of the theory of dialectic comes in the *Topics*. This has been one of the more neglected of his works in modern times. Previous generations have supplied the work with good commentaries, among which those of Alexander and Pacius are outstanding for the full exposition which each provides of the sense of Aristotle's words throughout the work. The most recent full-scale commentary is that of Waitz, published a hundred and thirty years ago, which also contains much valuable elucidation of the text, particularly in the first and eighth books.

But Waitz' work also marked a shift of scholarly interest away from the *Topics*. The amount of space which his commentary devotes to the *Topics* is only two thirds of that devoted to the *Posterior Analytics*, despite the fact that the former work is more than twice the length of the latter. While this is partly attributable to the fact that the text of the *Topics* presents fewer problems than that of most other Aristotelian works, it is also clear that Waitz felt that the *Topics* had little to contribute to the understanding of the core of Aristotle's philosophy.[1]

From then until recent years there has been comparatively little work on the book; and what there has been, has concerned itself predominantly with the historical question of the place of the *Topics* in the development of Aristotle's logical theories. The general tendency of this work has been to place the *Topics* at an early stage in a development which takes Aristotle from an interest in classification by genus and differentia by means of techniques which were practised in the Academy, to the discovery of the syllogism and of a theory of scientific method which is dependent on that discovery. Solmsen has been the most prominent among those who have argued a thesis of this sort, according to which the *Topics* represents an early stage of Aristotle's thought which was later to undergo revision in the *Analytics*; but a number of others, such as Maier, Stocks, and Ross, have also taken the view that the *Topics* antedates the *Analytics*. A further considerable influence in favour of this view

[1] cf. *Organon*, vol. 2, p. 439.

has been the work of Hambruch,[2] who drew attention to a number of similarities between theses found in the *Topics* and those found in the *Divisiones Aristoteleae*, which he believed to represent Academic doctrine,[3] and in Plato's later works. It should be noted that the attention of these scholars has been mainly directed towards the theory of the syllogism; and their work has been thought to have a bearing on the *Topics* because it embodies a double assumption about the syllogism. The first is that the *Topics* presents a theory of the syllogism which is clearly superseded by the theory of the *Prior Analytics*. This assumption has recently been challenged by Braun, who argues that the *Topics* presents a consistent account which does not need supplementation from the *Analytics*.[4] But this assumption has frequently been combined with a second, from which it ought to be distinguished; and this is that the theory of the *Prior Analytics* is the natural end to which Aristotle's logical theory tends, and that a work from which it is absent is therefore *ipso facto* earlier than one in which it is present.

The tendency of this historical work is well summarised by Chroust when he says: 'The *Topics*, for instance, is most certainly affected by the dialectics of Plato's late dialogues. Such a dependence, however, in no way detracts from the achievements of Aristotle who must still be credited with having progressed from (Platonic) dialectics to (Aristotelian) syllogistics.'[5] The assumption implicit in this remark is that the *Topics* represents a transitional stage in the development of Aristotle's logical thought, and that its chief value lies in the insight it might afford us into the nature of this development. It seems, then, that the studies of Aristotle's development have reinforced the tendency, which was already apparent in the distribution of space in Waitz' commentary, to regard the *Topics* as peripheral to the main area of Aristotle's philosophy.

There have been exceptions to this general pattern. Le Blond has recognised the importance of dialectic in Aristotle's theory of method and in his practice, as also have E. Weil and G. E. L. Owen. These scholars have stressed the importance which Aristotle assigns to dialectic in his theory of the discovery of the first principles of science; and they have also noted how his practice of prefacing the treatment of a question by arguing both sides of the case on the basis of current views conforms with this theoretical evaluation. Recently there have appeared some studies which seek to interpret the *Topics* as a work in its own right and not simply as intermediate

---

[2] *Logische Regeln der platonischen Schule in der aristotelischen Topik*, Berlin, 1904.
[3] p. 33.
[4] *Zur Einheit der aristotelischen 'Topik'*, Köln, 1959.
[5] 'The First Thirty Years of Modern Aristotelian Scholarship', p. 55.

between Platonic dialectic and Aristotelian syllogistic. There are the studies of de Pater on the theory of definition in the *Topics*, and of Braun on the unity of the *Topics*. The third Symposium Aristotelicum was devoted to the *Topics*; and J. Brunschwig is in process of producing a translation of the whole of the work, with a full introduction and extensive notes, in the Budé Series.[6] Another development of recent years which has made the study of the *Topics* easier is the publication of a number of valuable studies on Aristotle's formal logic. Chief among these have been the studies of Patzig, Ebbinghaus, and W. and M. Kneale, who have clarified both the achievements and the limitations of Aristotle's work in the *Prior Analytics* and have therefore made it easier to assess the contribution of the *Topics* to logical theory.[7]

The aim and argument of this book

These recent developments should be effective in bringing the *Topics* more to the attention of students of Aristotle and of Greek philosophy in general. But despite their value, our understanding of the *Topics* and of the place of dialectic in Aristotle's thought remains partial. Many of the recent studies have retained the assumption that the chief interest in the study of the *Topics* lies in the light which it may throw on works other than itself. While this is an undeniably valuable area of study, it is nevertheless one that skirts the question of the nature of the *Topics* as an exercise in its own right.

My aim in this study is to examine afresh the position of dialectic in Aristotle's thought. I have concentrated on the *theory* of dialectic because it seems to me that the importance of the use of dialectical techniques in the practice of Aristotle's investigations is sufficiently well recognised. What still remains to be done is to establish the position which dialectic occupies in Aristotle's theory of the forms of intellectual activity. I shall argue that dialectic occupies a distinct and important position in this theory, and that Aristotle takes a consistent view on this question throughout the various works in which it is discussed. In this argument a crucial part will be played by the distinction between the qualified and the unqualified forms of an expression, and by the use to which Aristotle puts this distinction in his analysis of a number of central philosophical concepts. I shall also argue that the *Topics* embodies a view of dialectic which is based on this analysis, and that the character of the work can only be properly appreciated when the importance of this analysis

---

[6] Volume I, covering the first four books, was published in 1967; at the time of writing Volume II, though promised, is still awaited.
[7] cf. esp. W. & M. Kneale, *The Development of Logic*, pp. 37–8, 41–3.

is understood. I propose, then, to undertake a radical reconsideration of the part played in Aristotle's thought by his concept of dialectic and by the *Topics*. The result will, I hope, be to make it clear that the study of these matters has a central place in any study of Aristotle's philosophy.

I am not directly concerned with questions of the relative chronology of Aristotle's works. I believe that before these questions can be embarked upon, it is necessary to obtain an accurate assessment of the absolute character of Aristotle's doctrines, and that in the case of dialectic this has not yet been done. Moreover, as I have said, I believe that premature answers to questions of chronology have assisted in keeping the *Topics* in the relative obscurity which at present surrounds it. Indirectly, however, my work has some bearing on the question of chronology, insofar as it argues that Aristotle's concept of dialectic as it is presented in the *Topics* is built upon certain analyses which were developed by Aristotle himself and are not to be found in the work of the Academy. Thus my work challenges the assumption that the *Topics* shows an Aristotle whose thought is as close to the world of the Academy as it is to the world of his own mature philosophy.[8]

I shall examine Aristotle's concept of dialectic from three points of view. In the next chapter I analyse the scattered remarks on dialectic which are to be found in the *Metaphysics*. This is the work which most comprehensively sets forth Aristotle's views on the relations between the various forms of intellectual activity; and I argue that the *Metaphysics* gives an account of the connection and distinction between dialectic and the sciences, including particularly the universal science of ontology, which is both philosophically coherent and consistent with what he says on this question in the logical works. My analysis of these texts depends upon certain philosophical theses which are examined and developed in the third chapter. Here I advance an account of the relation between human faculties and their objects which is, I maintain, of fundamental importance to the understanding of wide areas of Aristotle's thought and also of considerable value in the adjudication between the rival claims of conflicting metaphysical theories. I start with his brief but extremely suggestive discussion of the nature of the object of wish in the *Nicomachean Ethics*; and then I argue that it is possible to discern parallel elements in his analysis of the intellectual faculties and their objects. On the basis of the features of Aristotle's thought

---

[8] The assumption enjoys very wide currency. For a clear instance, cf. P. M. Huby, 'The Date of Aristotle's *Topics* and its Treatment of the Theory of Ideas', p. 76: 'It is clear that most of the terms used and the logical presuppositions found in the *Topics* were already current in the Academy and not Aristotle's invention.'

which I extract from these discussions, I argue that dialectic has a special and most important place among the modes of studying the world as Aristotle orders them. These results are confirmed by his comments in the *Topics* on the nature of the enterprise on which he is engaged. It emerges that his conception of dialectic, and the metaphysical theory within which it is located, must be sharply distinguished from the characteristic tendencies of Plato's thinking. In the final chapter I consider in detail certain features of the discussion of definition in the *Topics*. My argument here is that when the views expressed in the *Topics* are compared with what Aristotle has to say on the same issues in other works, and when the strategies which govern the discussions are considered, the practice of the *Topics* conforms well with the theory of dialectic for which I have argued in the preceding two chapters. The peculiar features of the discussion of definition in the *Topics* are of the sort which would be expected to occur in a work on dialectic as opposed to other modes of intellectual enterprise.

The general outcome, then, of the three rather diverse investigations which form the three main chapters of this book, is a view of the nature and function of dialectic which places it firmly in the centre of the mature Aristotle's thought. It may be helpful to anticipate the detailed argument by giving a very abstract statement of the concept of dialectic which will be set forth.

Dialectic must be distinguished from the sciences in that it does not work with any set view of reality. In this it is opposed both to the many special sciences and to the universal science of ontology, although it does share with the latter, against the special sciences, lack of restrictedness as to the scope of its operations. But what marks off the sciences from dialectic is that they embody a correct view of reality: this is true both of the special sciences, each of which has among its foundations an awareness of the real nature of some particular department of what there is, and of the universal science which takes as its basic concept Substance – the real nature of Reality itself. Dialectic, by contrast, should not embody any view of reality – neither a correct one, which would assimilate it to scientific ontology and would also blunt its effectiveness, nor an incorrect one, which will produce error in the sciences which dialectic serves.

This account of the relation between dialectic, science, and reality may be explained in terms of a more basic metaphysical doctrine of the relation between human faculties and their objects. If we are to allow scope for the distinction between expert and inexpert use of faculties, this can be done by saying that the objects of the expert's faculty are those things which *really are* what the objects of others' – inexperts' – faculties only *seem to be*. We must recognise that the object of a faculty takes two forms: it can be qualified by reference to the person or group for whom it is the object, or it can be free from such qualification, absolute. Only in the latter case does it possess the universality which is the condition of science. But if we are to give a satisfactory account of intellectual progress, both forms of objects of faculties must be taken into account. For it is *our* faculties that are engaged in this progress; and any account of the matter which ignores this will run into paradox. Accordingly the notion of *foundations* of understanding must incorporate the distinction between the unqualified object of understanding and the object of *each person*'s understanding. It is a contingent matter whether or not this distinction is present in the case of any given person. But in principle the distinction must be upheld as a basis for the difference between expert and inexpert performances. The unqualified objects of a faculty – and only these – are real: the objects which have to be qualified by reference to a specific exercise of the faculty are not real, although the exercises of the faculties which are directed towards them are no less real for that. Science is concerned with the real; and so its foundations must be without qualification more intelligible than what is explained on the basis of them. But there are other forms of intellectual exercise which accommodate uses of the human faculties which are other than expert; and these exercises are concerned with the qualified objects of the faculties as well as with the unqualified. One of these exercises is dialectic. It takes as its foundations what is *relatively* more intelligible than what is to be explained – relatively, that is, to the faculties of the audience of the explanation. In this way dialectic is the essential tool in the preliminary work which precedes the establishment of a complete science.

We must start with the objects as each is presented to our individual faculties, objects which will differ with the individuals who apprehend them. The faculties are engaged scientifically when these differences between individuals have been eliminated and the object is the same for all faculties which are directed towards it. Dialectic is the activity which effects the passage from the pre-scientific to the scientific use of the faculties. For dialectic, unlike the sciences, embraces both forms of the objects of faculties, and this explains the crucial and unique part which dialectic has to play in the investigation of things.

This is the thesis which I shall argue. It shows dialectic to play a central part in Aristotle's thought; and it is based on insights and analyses which Aristotle originated.

2

DIALECTIC AND THE WORKS OF ARISTOTLE

One of Aristotle's most important contributions to human thought was the idea that demarcation lines can be drawn between the different departments of expertise and that nothing is thereby lessened in the expertise of each distinct expert. In this his opposition to Plato is fundamental. For Plato believed that to know anything in the fullest sense it is necessary to know everything; he thought that any science or skill which is partial in its scope has only a limited claim to the title not simply of *universal* science but of *science*. He shows this belief not only in the *Republic*, where he argues that dialectic is the highest form of intellectual activity and is universal in its scope[1] but also in the late *Philebus*, where dialectic is distinguished from other forms of intellectual activity in purity and precision and also in having no *particular* subject-matter.[2]

Plato's attitude in this matter is a particular instance of his more general predilection for the one rather than the many. In the case of any plurality of instances, where each instance is partial in that it differs from the other instances and thus does not exhaust the nature of the collected whole of which the instances are part, Plato attaches *reality* not to any of the particular instances but rather to something which possesses all of the nature of which they possess a part. So also with sciences and skills it is the universal science, which is concerned not with some but with all the things that there are, which alone has the claim to be called *real* science. Further, Plato believed that all realities (the Forms) are joined by the Form of Good to form a unified whole, and that the nature of science is essentially linked to the nature of the reality which it studies;[3] and so he concluded that the synoptic science which he called dialectic was *the* science of reality, since it alone studies reality as it really is.

While Aristotle has many criticisms to make against Plato in the many contexts where Plato's preference for the one against the many manifests itself, it is his criticism of the Platonic notion of the

[1] 531d–534e, 537c.
[2] 55d–59e; cf. 57b5–7, 'different skills with different subject-matters'; cf. also *Soph.* 257c7–257d2.
[3] cf. *Timaeus* 29b–29c: 'So it must be determined concerning the representation and its exemplar in the following way, that the accounts are of the same character as the subjects which they expound.'

unity of science which perhaps more than anything else shapes the character of his philosophical method.[4] Since Aristotle takes over the name 'dialectic' which Plato had used to characterise his notion of science, and himself uses this same name for a *particular form* of intellectual activity which is not to be equated with the whole of intellectual activity, this makes the study of Aristotle's concept of dialectic particularly important if we wish to understand the nature of the contrast between Plato and Aristotle in this respect. Just as Plato and Aristotle are concerned with the same question when they give their very different answers as to the nature of reality, so also the very different accounts which the two philosophers give of the nature and value of dialectic are nevertheless concerned to provide answers to the same questions. In the case of both philosophers the problem from which they start is: To what extent can intellectual advance be achieved by the method of question and answer? The question is put in compressed form purposely, because behind it lie suppositions which were rather different for each of the two philosophers. For both of them it was a matter of experience that there was pedagogic value in the question and answer debate,[5] and equally both were aware that discipline had to be exercised in the performance of such debates if dialectic were not to degenerate into eristic.[6] However, while for Plato it was axiomatic that intellectual advance could be achieved by such debates if they were conducted according to certain rules, for Aristotle the fact of the pedagogic value and the existence of the safeguards did not in themselves guarantee intellectual advance. Aristotle distinguished things which are more intelligible absolutely from things which are more intelligible to us,[7] and this distinction represents a recognition of two senses in which something can be said to increase our understanding. The explanation may contain elements which are absolutely more intelligible than that which is to be explained, or elements which are only more intelligible to some particular person or group of people. Consequently Aristotle has the means of contrasting the genuinely and absolutely explanatory with what *people may find* explanatory; and the complexity of the situation can be seen from the fact that, according to the Aristotelian distinction between the two forms of intelligibility, one could speak of someone's, indeed of most people's, understanding being advanced by explanations which nonetheless are not genuinely explanatory. If this sounds para-

[4] cf. G. E. L. Owen, *The Platonism of Aristotle*, pp. 139–45.

[5] Plato *Meno* 80–6; Aristotle *Top.* A2.

[6] cf. G. Ryle, *New Essays on Plato and Aristotle*, pp. 55–8.

[7] *Ta gnōrimōtera haplōs* and *ta gnōrimōtera hēmin.* This distinction is found not only in the treatises but also in the fragments; cf. *De Philosophia* fr. 8 (Ross, *Fragmenta*, p. 76), where divine things are said to be 'most clear in their own nature but obscure and dim to us'.

doxical, we should consider the case of the man who finds Democritean reasoning for the existence of atoms more illuminating than that of a modern physicist; it is reasonable to say of such a man that the matter is explained *to him* by something other than the real explanation.

The question, then, with which Aristotle, like Plato, is faced when he considers the nature and value of dialectic is an ambiguous one and one of which he recognises the ambiguity. Consequently our comment on Aristotle's answer will have to recognise this ambiguity, and it will have to consider to which of the two possible interpretations of the sense of this question any answer which can be extracted from Aristotle's comments corresponds.

Metaphysics B *and* Γ: *the problem of dialectic and its resolution*

I start with a review of the evidence which the *Metaphysics* can contribute on this question; for a consistent picture can be extracted from all the remarks on dialectic in this work, and the *Metaphysics*, of all Aristotle's works, is that in which he discusses most comprehensively the relations between the different forms of intellectual activity.[8]

At *Met.* B1, 995b18–27, he presents one of the problems (*aporiai*) which must be examined before one can embark on the study of the principles of beings:

Whether the study is concerned only with substance or also with the essential attributes of substances; and in addition to these, concerning same and other and similar and dissimilar and contrariety, and concerning prior and posterior and all the other things of this sort which the dialecticians try to examine basing their examination on plausible views alone, whose job is it to study all these? – and in addition all the essential attributes of these very things, and not only the nature of each of them but also indeed whether one thing has one contrary.

We shall comment on this rambling text at length. Ross[9] regards the passage as presenting a single *aporia*: he justifies this view by a brief appeal to the fact that in the discussions of the difficulty in *Met* Γ2 the objects of the dialectician's study – Same, Other etc. – are treated as *per se* attributes of being *qua* being. However, whatever the terms of the solution of the difficulty as it is presented in Γ2, it should nevertheless be noted that the dialecticians are *explicitly* associated only with Same, Other etc.; and the suggestion

---

[8] Here and in what follows I use the expression 'intellectual activity' to cover practical and productive skills as well as theoretical knowledge, as Aristotle uses *dianoia* in *Met.* E1, 1025b25; cf. *EN* Z2, 1139a1.

[9] *Metaphysics*, vol. I, pp. 222, 224.

conveyed by the words 'and in addition to these' (l.20) is that the dialecticians would not at least have described *themselves* as concerned with the *per se* attributes of substances. The comment that the dialecticians conduct their enquiries only on the basis of plausible views is in full agreement with what Aristotle says elsewhere about the nature of dialectic.[10]

The extended presentation of the *aporia* at *Met.* B2, 997a25–34, proceeds entirely within terms of the distinction between substances and their attributes. There is no mention of the things which were said in B1 to belong to the dialectician's concern. The dilemma proceeds on the assumption that the study whose nature is being debated in *Met.* B conforms to the model of science which is established in the *Posterior Analytics*, according to which (*a*) both the subject and its attributes fall under the same science[11] and (*b*) demonstrative science (*apodeixis*) is not capable of establishing the *nature* (*ti esti*) of anything.[12] These criteria for being a science are used in the development of the dilemma as follows: (i) the science of *ousia* must study the attributes of *ousia* (by *a*), (ii) there can be no science of *ousia* (by *b*) and therefore either no science of its attributes or one which studies the attributes but not their subject (which conflicts with *a*).[13] *Ousia* is the word which I have translated 'substance' in the passage of *Met.* B1 quoted above; but here I leave the word transliterated since in what follows I shall discuss the dangers of oversimplification which this translation brings.

Ross's comment[14] on this passage seriously underestimates the

---

[10] *Top.* A1, 100a29–30; *SE* 2, 165b3–4.

[11] *An. Post.* A7, 75b1; *Met.* B2, 997a19–20.

[12] *An. Post.* B7, 92b35–8. These lines conclude a lengthy polemic against the view that definitions can be demonstrated, which has occupied *An. Post.* B3–7. The polemic is based on theses of Aristotle's own devising, such as that immediate connections are indemonstrable (93b21–8, cf. 72b18–20); and so Bonitz (*Metaphysica, ad. loc.*) is wrong to describe *Met.* 997a31 as expressing a generally held view. Rather, at this point Aristotle is working with an *endoxon* of his own.

[13] The version in *Met.* K1, 1059a29–34, uses the same considerations about the nature of demonstrative science to develop the dilemma in a rather different form. The argument first establishes that the study of the attributes, being apodeictic, cannot also study the *ousiai*, and *then* argues that (i) if wisdom (*sophia*) is apodeictic, it must be concerned with the attributes and not the *ousiai*, (ii) if it is concerned with what is fundamental, it must study the *ousiai* and not their attributes. The difference between the two accounts is that in K1 the notion of *apodeixis* is slightly less central to the dilemma than it is in B2. Since the solution of this problem depends on freeing the notion of a science from the rigid criteria which are imposed by the model of *apodeixis*, the greater dominance of this model in the B2 version gives it the appearance of being a more finished presentation of the problem.

[14] *Metaphysics*, vol. I, p. 231.

nature of the difficulty. His solution is that 'Wisdom defines substances and demonstrates their attributes'. He has perhaps been
misled by 997a27–30, where the contrast between substances and
their attributes is illustrated by the contrast between certain mathe-
matical subjects – such as Lines and Planes – which are assumed for
the sake of the illustration to be substances, and their attributes.
But, even if we assume that such subjects are substances, the case of
these subjects and their attributes provides no more than an illustration of the problematic case with which Aristotle is concerned,
viz. the case in which the subject of the supposed science is Substance itself (not things which are substances). In the case of lines,
what cannot be demonstrated is their substantiality; but this does
not prevent them from being a subject of demonstration in respect of
other things that are true of them (their attributes). But with Substance itself we seem to be dealing with a subject which is essentially
incapable of acting as a subject of demonstration. Aristotle's theory
of demonstration incorporates an opposition between the notions of
substance and attribute which is exploited in the dilemma of *Met.*
B2. If we suppose that, while the nature of Substance is indemonstrable, nevertheless its attributes can be demonstrated, we are
ignoring this opposition or effectively supposing that among its
attributes are some which contradict the nature of their subject.
This would be like supposing that among the attributes of lines
there are some which cannot be linear in character and that these
are demonstrably true of their subject.

The solution to the problem of *Met.* B1–2 is given in Γ2. The
chapter opens with an analysis of the word 'being'. This shows
it to be neither straightforwardly univocal nor straightforwardly
equivocal: rather, it must be analysed into a primary sense and into
secondary senses which can be explained only by reference to the
primary sense. In the primary sense the word is used of substances;
in the secondary senses it is used of things which are logically
parasitic on substances, for example by being qualifications or
productive of them. The primary sense of 'being' *is* univocal, and
it functions as a central core of meaning in all the various applications which occur according to the secondary senses.[15] Consequently
the multiplicity of the word's senses does not prevent there being a
unitary study of all beings.[16] This study covers not only being but
also Unity, which may differ in intension but is identical in extension to being,[17] and also certain 'species of unity', such as Same and
Similar, which can be reduced to unity in some way not here
specified,[18] and also the contraries of these species, such as Different,

[15] 1003b5–10.   [16] 1003b11–16.
[17] 1003b22–33.   [18] 1003b33–7.

Dissimilar, Unequal, since contraries fall under the same study.[19] At 1004a31–5 we have an explicit reference to the problem of B1, and from this point to 1004b26 the argument seeks to specify the relation between dialectic and philosophy.[20]

Both philosophy and dialectic are concerned with everything that there is; and this explains why the objects of the dialectician's concern should also be proper objects of the philosopher's concern as attributes of beings in respect of their being. Just as subjects have various attributes in respect of their being numbers (oddness, equality etc.), so also they have various attributes simply in respect of their being *things*. These attributes are not restricted to any determinate type of subject (as oddness is to numbers) but may be true of anything.[21] On the distinction between dialectic and philosophy two points are made. Firstly, they differ in the results that they can produce. Dialectic can only be tentative where philosophy is scientific: that is, negatively dialectic can demolish claims to knowledge[22] but positively it is unable itself to produce knowledge.[23] Secondly, others who are concerned with the *per se* attributes of beings (which are part of the philosopher's concern) fail to practise philosophy insofar as they have no appreciation of the nature of *ousia*, which is prior to these attributes.[24] These other thinkers are not here called dialecticians; and it may, in any case, be doubted whether it is legitimate to use a remark of Aristotle's about *dialecticians* as evidence for his views about *dialectic*. Against this, however, a comparison with 995b20–7 makes it certain that the thinkers who are castigated here are to be identified with those who are there called 'the dialecticians'.[25] As to whether the practice of these people is relevant to the question of Aristotle's own ideas about dialectic, the remark at *Met.* K3, 1061b7–10 – 'dialectic and sophistic are concerned with the attributes of things which are, but not insofar as they are nor with what is to the extent to which it is'

---

[19] 1004a9–31. The other items mentioned in B1 as falling within the dialectician's concern are also included – 'opposite', 1004a20, 'prior' and 'posterior', 1005a16.

[20] By 'philosophy' here and in the remainder of this chapter I mean the activity which Aristotle calls '*philosophia*' i.e. the activity which he is attempting to describe and practise in the *Metaphysics* (cf. Γ2, 1004b21; A9, 992a33). I also sometimes use the expression 'scientific ontology' to designate this activity, for reasons which I hope the context makes clear.

[21] The relation of these attributes to their subjects is characterised in different ways in different places. They are called *pathē* (1004b5), *eidē* (1003b34), *huparchonta* (1005a14), *sumbebēkota* (1061b4). These variations appear to be irrelevant to the present doctrine.

[22] cf. *SE* 11, 172a17–27.

[23] 1004b22–6.

[24] 1004b8–10; on this text see pp. 15–16 below.

[25] Compare 1004b3–4 with 995b26–7.

– strongly suggests that he would not draw any distinction between talk about dialecticians and talk about dialectic. This suggestion is strengthened when we see that immediately before, and in support of, his characterisation of dialectic as equal in scope but unequal in cognitive effect to philosophy Aristotle speaks of dialecticians (1004b17,19). Generally, Aristotle is inclined to minimise the difference between his own conception of the nature of a particular form of intellectual activity and the conceptions of that form of activity as revealed in his predecessors' work.[26]

So when Aristotle speaks of an inadequacy on the part of those who have previously considered the attributes of beings *qua* beings, we may expect his comments on this inadequacy to reveal something positive about his conception of the proper nature of dialectic. In Γ2 Aristotle is concerned to show that (*a*) the activity of the dialectician does not amount to philosophy, despite the dialecticians' belief to the contrary, but (*b*) what the dialectician is concerned with does form part of the philosopher's concern. Both (*a*) and (*b*) are necessary elements in Aristotle's defence of his conception of the universal study of Being against the main alternative contender for this title, Plato's conception of dialectic as the super-science. (*a*) is in effect the statement of Aristotle's opposition to the alternative position, but (*b*) is necessary to preclude the charge that Aristotle has ignored what is valuable in his opponents' account and simply set up an alternative of his own which may have as much, but not necessarily any more, than the opposing account to recommend it. In fact, Aristotle's procedure here is an example of the method which he uses in a wide variety of contexts – that of showing how previous accounts of some matter have some value but also contain some error, so that they cannot be accepted *in toto*: by this means he prevents the continuance of these accounts as *rivals* to his own by incorporating into his own account what is of value in them. In the case of dialectic Aristotle argues that previous thinkers had a correct idea as to which characters are as wide in extension as being and should, therefore, fall within the study of everything that there is. But he maintains that they had an inadequate notion of being; and thus he is unable to allow that their activity should be called philosophy, which, as the study of everything that there is, depends fundamentally on a proper idea of what it is for anything to be. With his demonstration that the analysis of the concepts –

26 Thus in *Phys.* A (184b17, 186a20, 187a12) the Eleatics are denied the title of 'natural philosophers (*phusikoi*)' because they argued against the possibility of motion, although it seems clear that they would have regarded themselves as engaged in the same kind of study as those whom Aristotle is prepared to call 'natural philosophers'. Aristotle counts as his *predecessors* in a study those for whom the questions to be investigated, even if not the answers, were the same as his own.

same etc. – with which the dialecticians were concerned follows the same pattern as the analysis of being (an analysis which Aristotle originated), he is further able to show that a proper understanding of these concepts was not available to those who supposed that the activities of dialectic and philosophy were identical.

This argument, then, states that dialectic is a non-scientific activity which should not be confused with philosophy, although some have been misled by the identity of scope between the two activities into making this confusion. The reason for their being so misled was their failure to appreciate the nature and fundamental character of *ousia*. From this we may infer that there is a proper conception of dialectic, and a proper way to practise it, which does not confuse it with philosophy, and that when dialectic is practised properly no explicit account of the nature of being is necessary and no particular view on this question should be taken. To the first of these inferences it may be objected that the argument in Γ2 no more shows that there is a proper way of practising dialectic than arguments at some future time for a science of e.g. predictive astronomy would show that there is a *proper* way of practising astrology (i.e. the art as it was conceived in ancient and mediaeval times): either there is no proper way to practise astrology or the only proper way is the method of predictive astronomy. Equally an account of the proper way to practise scientific ontology, so far from implying that there is a proper way to practise dialectic, suggests rather that either there is no proper way of practising dialectic or that the proper way is that of scientific ontology. However, to attempt to reduce dialectic to ontology is to make the same mistake as those whom Aristotle is here attacking, who regarded the proper way of doing philosophy as identical with the proper way of doing dialectic; and to argue from the distinction between philosophy and dialectic that there is no proper way of doing dialectic is to ignore the third way of universal activity mentioned here, sophistic, which *is* the sham member of the trio and the counterpart of astrology. No emphasis is placed on the distinction between dialectic and sophistic in *Met.* Γ2, but his characterisation of these two forms of activity recalls contexts where they are emphatically distinguished.[27] To the second of the inferences above it may be objected that Aristotle's words show rather that it is important for the correct practice of dialectic that the nature and primacy of *ousia* should be recognised, and not, as stated above, that the dialectician should take no particular view on the nature of *ousia*. But I should argue that this interpretation is akin to that which reduces the proper practice of dialectic to the proper practice of scientific ontology. The activity which recognises that

[27] e.g. *SE* 11, 171b6–9, where sophistic is emphatically asserted to be sham dialectic.

the universal characters – same etc. – are attributes of Being *qua* being and treats them in accordance with the analysis of Being which reveals the primacy of substance, is none other than philosophy; and so dialectic must be distinguished from philosophy precisely in failing to embody this recognition. The distinction can hardly reside *simply* in the tentative, as opposed to scientific, character of dialectic, since there is no reason to suppose that, were the dialectician in possession of the analysis of Being which guarantees the scientific character of philosophy,[28] his activity would be any less scientific than the philosopher's. Rather, it is the failure of his activity to reflect the presence of such an analysis which gives it its non-scientific character.[29]

On the other hand, if dialectic should not reflect the correct ontological insights which characterise philosophy, still less should it be burdened with some incorrect ontology, for example with the Platonic ontology which, as I noted above,[30] is directly responsible for what Aristotle believed to be Plato's mistaken view of the nature of dialectic. There is surely an allusion to this point in the remark that the dialecticians 'understand nothing about *ousia*'.[31] I remarked earlier that care is needed in the translation of this word. The convention of translating it by 'substance' has good reason and raises no problem in many passages of Aristotle. But it must be borne in mind that the Aristotelian doctrine which is reflected in his use of the word, itself represents a refinement of a more familiar and primitive notion which is best seen in the translations 'reality' or 'real being'. Other philosophers are credited with speaking about 'reality' but not about 'substance'. Accordingly there are a number of passages where it is more revealing to translate the word by 'reality' rather than by 'substance', although the latter translation is not completely inappropriate.[32] Such is the case with the present remark. When Aristotle says of other philosophers that they have no understanding of *ousia*, he is certainly saying that they have no awareness of his own notion of substance. But to leave it at that would be to obscure the connection between Aristotle's own ideas and those of other philosophers. He is also making the point that the others lacked a proper notion of reality, something with which both they and Aristotle are concerned. It is, of course, true that the Academy, for example, had its own ideas about the nature of reality;

---

[28] 1003b12–16.
[29] *Met.* K3, 1061b4–11, argues that dialectic and sophistic are not concerned with things *insofar as they are*: only philosophy embodies this concern.
[30] pp. 7–8.
[31] 1004b10.
[32] W. E. Charlton's comments on this point are useful (*Aristotle's Physics Books I and II*, pp. 56–7).

but the Academy lacked the Aristotelian notion of substance. Accordingly Aristotle can say that they had no *understanding* of reality, because they had no understanding of substance, which his own analysis had shown to be fundamental to the notion of reality. Consequently, although Aristotle's explicit point in 1004b8–10 is that previous thinkers were mistaken (because they had no notion of reality – i.e. of substance), in supposing their dialectical activity to be philosophical, his remarks hint at the further point that *their* notions of reality prevented their activities from being properly dialectical.

It will be seen that in *Met.* Γ2 there is no attempt to unravel the problem of B2 in accordance with the terms in which it is there developed: the notion of demonstrative science, which in B2 provides the grounds for the conflict of answers, receives no mention in Γ2. The short answer to this is that Aristotle is here implicitly rejecting the idea that it is a condition of any activity's being scientific that it conform to the model of demonstration: he does this explicitly in Γ3–4 when he argues that it is the task of philosophy to investigate the principles of reasoning,[33] and goes on to call the demand that if anything is to be established it must be demonstrated a mark of lack of education.[34] However, this short answer can be supplemented when we remember the complexity of the meaning of *ousia* to which I have referred – 'reality' and 'substance'. The *Analytics* is concerned with the notion of reality and argues that it is impossible to demonstrate a thing's definition – what it really is. *Met.* Γ2 employs the refined notion of reality, according to which it characterises one type of being – substance – and argues that it is by reference to substance that the being of all other types of thing is to be explained. Further, the notion of substance provides the explanation not only of the various modes of being which are enjoyed by the different types of thing, but also of the nature of the attributes of the things which are, insofar as they are (i.e. same, other etc.). So that which cannot be treated by demonstrative science according to the theory of science in the *Posterior Analytics* – *ousia* – is argued in *Met.* Γ2 to be that element in the notion of Being *qua* being which makes it possible for there to be a science of Being and its attributes at all. While there is no attempt in *Met.* Γ to counter the arguments by which in the *Analytics* the incompatibility of *ousia* and demonstrative science is urged, the emphasis on the central role of *ousia* in the science of ontology does look like a direct challenge to the argument with which the *Analytics* provides the opponent of ontology in *Met.* B2. This impression is reinforced when we note the pointed way in which the special attributes of Number *qua* number, which are readily admitted together with their subject to

[33] 1005b5–8.   [34] 1006a5–18.

be the subject-matter of a science in the *Analytics*, are introduced as an illustration of the idea that it is also possible for that which is, insofar as it is, to have special attributes.[35]

So on the basis of these passages in the *Metaphysics* we may say that dialectic is concerned with everything that there is, but not concerned with what it is for anything to be. It is this ontological neutrality of dialectic which makes it a non-scientific activity. For what is essential for scientific activity is an appreciation of some central concept which links all the particular items that fall within and make up the science. In the case of the study of the things that there are, the central concept is *ousia*; and it is this which dialectic lacks.

Metaphysics A *and* M: *Aristotle on Socratic and Platonic dialectic*

We get further confirmation that this was Aristotle's view of dialectic from two passages in which the notion of dialectic is employed to explain the origins of Plato's ontology.

In *Met.* A6, 987b29–33, he says that Plato differed from the Pythagoreans in setting numbers *apart* from the objects which they characterise; he explains that both this feature of Platonism and the introduction of Forms took place 'because of enquiry by arguments (for his predecessors took no part in dialectic)'. This is one of a number of passages in the *Metaphysics* where the development of Plato's ontology is associated with his interest in arguments;[36] and as Ross observes,[37] Aristotle was very probably influenced to make this judgement by *Phaedo* 100a. The method which Plato describes in this passage is that of 'enquiring into the truth of things by arguments';[38] and although it is not here called dialectic, this identification may surely be made.[39] The method involves the use of hypotheses, and after the description of its general character we are given an application of it to the problem of proving the soul's indestructibility. The hypothesis chosen as most likely to lead to this conclusion is that the Forms exist; and there commentators have generally been content to leave the matter, simply regarding the introduction of the Forms as an illustration, not an integral feature, of the hypothetical method.[40] However, examination of the text does in fact suggest a closer connection between the Forms and the hypothetical method. It must be remembered that the larger context

[35] Γ2, 1004b10–17.
[36] 1050b35, 1069a26–8, 1084b23–5.
[37] *Metaphysics*, vol. 1, pp. 172–3.
[38] *Phaedo* 99e5.
[39] Thus R. Robinson, *Plato's Earlier Dialectic*, p. 70.
[40] R. Robinson, p. 134: 'The hypothesis chosen is the theory of Ideas'.

for this passage is the need to investigate 'the ground of generation and destruction'[41] and this is reflected in the use of the word 'ground (*aitia*)' at 100b8 and 100c6–7 to express the relationship between hypothesis and whatever may be derived from it. Yet these passages, especially 100c6–7 – 'do you accept a ground of this type?' – suggest that Plato tended to regard mention of the Forms as essential to the sort of explanation which can be provided by the dialectical method. In the absence of any explicit statement about the relationship between the Forms and the method, there is no justification for speaking of more than a tendency to connect the two. But at least this much does seem justified, when we note that the Forms are produced as one sort of ground for an assertion and as such are to be set beside the other two sorts of ground (the mechanical sort used by Socrates' predecessors, and the Good) which have been considered previously in the discussion.[42] That this is how Aristotle regarded the matter, which is my principal concern, is suggested by the distinction, in his own theory of grounds (*aitiai*), of the sort of explanation which mentions the *form* of the subject from the sorts of explanation which mention the purpose (cf. the Good in the *Phaedo*) or the material constituents or the efficient cause of the subject (cf. the modes of explanation which are rejected in the *Phaedo*). G. E. L. Owen has noted the highly Platonic language which Aristotle sometimes uses to characterise the formal cause in expositions of the doctrine of the four causes;[43] and this lends further force to the suggestion that Aristotle's theory arose out of reflection on Plato's work in the same field. If this is so, of all the passages in which Plato discusses the nature of explanation *Phaedo* 96–100 is the one which most comprehensively foreshadows Aristotle's own theory.

We may say, then, that it is probable that Aristotle read *Phaedo* 100 as arguing that in addition to other sorts of explanation that can be given there is one sort that involves an appeal to the Forms. This is the sort of explanation that occurs when one considers some matter by means of arguments (*logoi*); that is to say, it is the sort of explanation that occurs when dialectic is employed. So, when Aristotle says in *Met.* A6 that certain peculiar features of Plato's ontology are to be explained by his employment of (and his predecessors' failure to employ) dialectic, his comment should be read against this background. What he says here accords with the comments on dialectic in *Met.* Γ2 which argued that although there is indeed a connection between dialectic and ontology, failure

---

[41] 95e9. [42] 96–99.
[43] 'Dialectic and Eristic in the Treatment of the Forms', p. 124; *Phys.* B3, 194b26–8, *Met.* Δ2, 1013a26–8, describe the formal cause as 'the form and exemplar'.

also to recognise the distinction between the two exercises will result in poor dialectic and incorrect ontology. For a clearer indication of how this is so we must turn to the more extended comments of *Met.* M4.

It will be useful to give in full the text of this complex passage:

1078b17   Socrates concerned himself with moral virtues and was the first to attempt to give universal definitions of these (for of the natural philosophers
20   Democritus only slightly touched on the matter, giving a sort of definition of hot and cold, and before him the Pythagoreans attached to numbers the definitions of a few things, for example of opportunity, justice and marriage. But he had good reason to look for the definition; for he sought to reason, and definition is the foundation of pieces of reasoning; for
25   dialectic was not yet at that time sufficiently strong to be capable of also examining contraries apart from the definition, and whether the study of contraries is the same; for there are two things which one would be right to ascribe to Socrates, inductive arguments and universal definitions; for these are both concerned with the
30   foundation of science). But Socrates did not make the universals or the definitions separate: it was they who separated them.

(*Met.* M4, 1078b17–31)

Commentators on this passage have tended to concentrate on the information which it provides about Socrates and the relationship between his ideas and those of Plato, at the expense of what it has to tell us about Aristotle's ideas on dialectic, reasoning and definition. An exception is P. Wilpert who argues that consideration of what is said in this passage should lead us to revise our ideas on Aristotle's valuation of dialectic. This study is a move in the right direction, but more remains to be done on the elucidation of what the passage has to tell us on this point.[44]

The main statement of the passage is clear; although Socrates was the first to seek universal definitions of moral virtues, he did not assign separate existence to the universals which he sought to define. But the train of argument within the long bracket is by no means clear; and of this the most difficult section, because it least obviously contributes to the argument, is the remark about dialectic in lines 25–7.

Lines 19–25 expand the claim of line 19 about Socrates' originality. He is contrasted with some of his predecessors in that while

---

[44] Wilpert, 'Aristoteles und die Dialektik', is mainly concerned with Aristotle's valuation of dialectic and with the relation between Aristotle's own contribution to the art and that of his predecessors. He has little to say on the argument of *Met.* M4 as such.

they in a limited sense (Democritus) or to a limited extent (the Pythagoreans) engaged in definition, he practised definition as a systematic response to his desire to reason. To justify this analysis of Socrates' motivation Aristotle appeals to the fact that definition is fundamental to reasoning (*sullogismos*). Although the grammatical form of this statement about definition presents it as an observation about Aristotle's own doctrine[45] rather than as an explicit statement of Socratic theory, nevertheless the evidence of Plato's dialogues indicates that we should probably regard it as a comment on Socrates' *reasons*, and not just his motives, for being concerned with definition.[46]

The sentences which follow continue with the justification for the original assertion that Socrates' concern with definitions was reasonable. In lines 25–7 we are told that in Socrates' time dialectical skill was not developed to the point that it was possible to study contraries independently of definitions. Although the connecting particle in line 25 indicates that this comment is intended as an explanation of the previous comments on the relationship between reasoning and definition, it is not clear with what justification Aristotle introduces *dialectic* at this point. Dialectic and reasoning are not equivalent notions for Aristotle, since not all reasoning is dialectical[47] and dialectic does not consist entirely of reasoning.[48] Further, even if it turns out that the character of Socratic argument is sufficiently similar to Aristotle's notion of dialectic to justify his using it in this analysis, there is still the difficulty that Aristotle's statement about dialectic appears to introduce a distinction – that between the study of contraries and the study of definitions – which is expressly said to be unavailable to the Socratic conception of dialectic. So the transition in Aristotle's argument from considerations of reasoning to considerations of dialectic raises two problems: (1) what sort of relation between dialectic and reasoning is being presupposed, and (2) is Aristotle fair to the historical facts in his comments here on the nature of dialectic?

The remarks in lines 27–9 have bearing on both these problems. These lines credit Socrates with the practice of inductive arguments and universal definition; and concern with the light which they

---

[45] The words are not in oratio obliqua, and the statement does, of course, represent Aristotle's own view; cf. *Met*. Z9, 1034a30–2.

[46] *Meno* 86d exhibits Socrates' reluctance to consider the attributes of a subject before establishing its definition.

[47] *Top*. A1, 100a25–100b26, the dialectical syllogism is contrasted with other forms of syllogism, viz. the apodeictic and the eristic; *SE* 2 contrasts dialectical arguments with didactic, peirastic and eristic arguments, all of which are syllogistic.

[48] *Top*. A12 distinguishes two forms of dialectical argument, one of which is reasoning (*sullogismos*) and the other is induction (*epagōgē*).

throw on the historical Socrates has diverted attention away from the question of their connection with the preceding argument. Universal definition has already been mentioned and indeed it is this feature of Socrates' practice which occasions the whole of this section of the argument; but the mention of induction is new. Nevertheless, it is natural that Aristotle should speak of induction after mentioning dialectic, since, as was noted above, dialectical argument takes the two forms of reasoning (*sullogismos*) and induction. This division of arguments is, moreover, peculiar to dialectic. In the theory of scientific demonstration induction is opposed to apodeictic syllogism, and the latter alone has a place *within* scientific activity, although the importance of induction as a *preliminary* to scientific activity is, of course, recognised.[49] Since Aristotle has already argued that definition was fundamental to Socrates' conception of reasoning, the latter's concern with induction and definition accords with the pattern of dialectical argument which Aristotle presents in *Top.* A12. So we can say in answer to the first problem – what sort of relation between dialectic and reasoning is being presupposed? – that Aristotle regards Socrates' reasoning as dialectical reasoning and supports this by appealing to the fact that Socrates used the two types of argument, induction and syllogism, which are characteristic of dialectic alone.

However, this brings us to the second problem – is Aristotle justified in explaining Socrates' practice in reasoning by appeal to features of dialectic which expressly did not characterise Socratic argument, even if that manner of argument be allowed, because of certain similarities between it and Aristotelian dialectic, the title of dialectic? The evidence other than this passage for believing that Aristotle considered Socrates a dialectician consists of a single passage in the *SE*[50] which appeals to Socrates' practice in question and answer debate to support Aristotle's choice of the matter which he treats in the *Topics* and *SE*. But though this evidence is slight, it is extremely important since the method of question and answer is a fundamental feature of Aristotelian dialectic.[51] It is the fact

[49] *An. Post.* A18, 81a39–b1 – 'we learn either by induction or by demonstration'. *An. Pr.* B23 opens with the contrast between syllogism and induction (68b13–14), but then speaks of 'the syllogism from induction' (68b15) and attempts to show that inductive arguments can be put in syllogistic form. But as Aristotle recognises (68b27–9), this can only be done where we have reviewed all the particulars and the induction is *perfect*. Perfect induction, however, is not what Aristotle ordinarily means by 'induction', nor is it the sort of induction which we see Socrates practising. Ross (*Analytics*, pp. 486–7) is correct in calling this chapter 'a *tour de force*'.

[50] *SE* 34, 183b7–8.

[51] *Top.* Θ 1, 155b1–16. This is Aristotle's justification for saying that peirastic is a part of dialectic, *SE* 11, 171b3–6.

that dialectic proceeds by asking questions rather than making statements which distinguishes it from scientific demonstration.[52] Consequently Aristotle is justified in using the word 'dialectic' to describe an activity of Socrates which shares a feature which is fundamental to the activity of his own which the word designates.

It may be thought that this latter point is sufficient justification for the introduction of dialectic to the argument of *Met.* M4 and that it is unnecessary for the explanation of the argument to appeal to the exclusively dialectical character of induction. But this overlooks the fact that Aristotle is trying to show how Socrates' concern with definitions was a natural result of his interest in argument; and to do this he must refer not to the *manner* (i.e. question and answer) in which Socrates conducted his arguments but rather to the *forms* of argument which he practised. Aristotle nowhere suggests that it would not be *possible* to put the premisses of the syllogisms of scientific demonstration in question form,[53] merely that to do so would be to fail to recognise the essentially didactic nature of scientific demonstration. On the other hand, he does insist, except in *An. Pr.* B23 which, as I have noted,[54] tends to belie its own argument, that there is no room for induction in demonstration. So independent considerations require us to follow Aristotle's explicit reasoning in *Met.* M4 in regarding the appeal to Socrates' concern with induction as responsible for the characterisation of his method of argument as dialectical.

The final part of Aristotle's argument for the reasonableness of Socrates' concern with definition comes in lines 29–30 with the statement that both induction and universal definition are fundamental to the securing of knowledge. Here Aristotle is alluding to the doctrine, which is prominent throughout his works, that science must start from certain elementary propositions which are its foundations.[55] The doctrine receives its main exposition in the *Posterior Analytics*. Briefly, it says that there are certain starting-points in any scientific enterprise which are essential preliminaries to demonstration but are themselves indemonstrable, and that these

---

[52] *SE* 10, 171b1–2.

[53] On this, cf. E. Kapp, *Greek Foundations of Traditional Logic*, especially chapter one. Kapp's argument is that the language which Aristotle uses to expound his theory of syllogistic in the *Prior Analytics* shows clear traces of an earlier logical theory, out of which the syllogistic grew, according to which securing a proof essentially involved obtaining agreement to premisses put in question form. While the general thesis may not be acceptable, Kapp's evidence supports the present point, that there would be no loss in logical character if the premisses of scientific demonstration were put in question form.

[54] p. 21 n. 49 above.

[55] cf. Bonitz *Index* 111b58–112a40 for a collection of passages where '*archē*' bears this sense.

starting-points are the common axioms[56] and the existence of the subject (e.g. number) of the science and the meanings of the words which designate its attributes.[57] With the philosophical credentials of this doctrine I am not here concerned. Aristotle devotes little space to any critical examination of it;[58] and the difficulties which it causes Aristotle in *Met.* Γ have been noted by J. R. Bambrough.[59] The point which I do wish to make here is that what is said in lines 29–30 recalls the argument of *Top.* A2, 101a36–101b4, that one of the uses to which dialectic may be put is the examination of the foundations of each of the particular sciences. Such an examination cannot be conducted within the discipline of any of the sciences since this would be to ignore the fundamental character of the foundations; otherwise there would be no need for foundations. But dialectic is specially, if not uniquely,[60] suited to perform the examination; for its scope is not restricted to some particular area of study, and it is not, therefore, precluded from studying the foundations of the sciences either by their being *its* foundations or by being the study of some particular area other than that covered by any given particular science and its foundations. Induction, as I have already said, has no place *within* the particular demonstrative science, and for this reason it cannot be ranked among the foundations (*archai*) of the science. On the other hand, as G. E. L. Owen has argued,[61] the procedure of basing the investigation of a problem on a review of current views (*endoxa*), to which Aristotle alludes in *Top.* A2 and which he uses so frequently at the beginning of his investigations of particular problems, may reasonably be called inductive. The assumption embodied in reviews of this type is that each of the views represents part of the correct answer to the problem but not the whole of it; and so the passage from examination of these views to acquisition of the true answer may be likened to the passage from the particular to the universal. When we note that Aristotle in lines 29–30 describes induction and universal definition as '*concerned with* the foundation of science' rather than 'foundations of science', i.e. as external, though not irrelevant, to the sciences, the probability that he is alluding to the sort of consideration which is advanced in *Top.* A2, i.e. to features of *dialectical*

---

[56] *An. Post.* 76a38, 77a26–31.

[57] 76b3–22.

[58] His reasons for maintaining it can be seen from the arguments in *An. Post.* A3 and A19–22 which use the idea of fixed starting-points of demonstration to show that scientific knowledge is not circular and is finite.

[59] 'Unanswerable Questions', *Aristotelian Society Supplementary Volume* XL, 1966, p. 165.

[60] *Top.* 101b2 – such an examination is 'peculiar to or most appropriate to dialectic'.

[61] '*Tithenai ta phainomena*' in *Aristote Et Les Problèmes De Méthode*, p. 87.

argument, is strengthened. Once again, then, we find confirmation in general consideration of Aristotle's theory of science for the suggestion conveyed by the form of the argument, that the introduction of the notion of dialectic is essential for Aristotle's justification of Socrates' procedure.

It will be useful to summarise the results of this discussion by presenting the argument of 1078b23–30 in tabular form. The premisses in square brackets are not explicit in the text.

1078b29–30   (1) Induction and universal definition are fundamental to science.

   b27–9   (2) Socrates practised both of these.

          [(3) Dialectic explores the fundamentals of science.]

          [(4) Dialectical argument takes the two forms of induction and reasoning.]

   b24–5   (5) Definition is fundamental to reasoning.

   b24   (6) Socrates sought to reason.

   b24–7   (7) Dialectic in Socrates' time was unable to proceed without concerning itself with definitions.

  b23 ∴ (8) Socrates, with good reason, sought definitions. There is a temptation to insert between (2) and (3) a further premiss – 'Socrates practised dialectic'. But I have argued[62] that any reasons other than those contained in the premisses above for this insertion are external to the structure of the argument. The argument can stand without them; and they would simply reinforce the conclusion, which can in fact be derived from the stated premisses, that the similarities between Socratic argument and Aristotelian dialectic justify Aristotle's application of theses which hold good of his dialectic to an account of the genesis of Socratic argument.

Formulation of the argument shows how important are the three premisses which mention dialectic. Only (7) is explicit in the text, but I have argued that both (3)[63] and (4)[64] represent basic Aristotelian doctrine on the nature of dialectic. The importation of these two premisses into the body of the argument is essential; for without them premisses (1) and (2) would be otiose, and premiss (7) would lack justification for its place in the argument. But if we remove premisses (1), (2) and (7) from the argument and retain only premisses (5) and (6), we are left with an argument which provides Socrates not merely with *good* reason but with *unassailably* good reason for being concerned with definition. This would be a travesty of Aristotle's argument, as is clear not only from the fact that premiss (7) *is* in the text and clearly introduces some limitation on the absolute validity of Socrates' procedure, but also from the fact that by talking of the 'good reason' for a move in a person's argument here, as in many other passages, Aristotle intends to convey

[62] pp. 21–2 above.   [63] pp. 22–4 above.   [64] pp. 20–1 above.

that there is a certain lack of support in Socrates' premises for the conclusion which he draws from them.[65]

As Aristotle represents it, it is possible to go a long way in the justification of Socrates, but not all the way. We have to stop short when we realise the inadequacy of the Socratic notion of dialectic, an inadequacy which is revealed in his assumption that dialectical reasoning *necessarily* concerns itself with definitions. Thus it is the notion of dialectic which shows both the justification and the lack of it for Socrates' interests. If Socrates had not practised dialectic, he would not have practised the two forms of argument, induction and reasoning, which are essential to the acquisition of scientific knowledge; but if he had practised dialectic *properly*, he would not have attempted to make definition the basis of his reasoning. As I have said, if we wish to understand the opposition between Plato and Aristotle in the theory of the organisation of scientific investigation, the contrast between their notions of dialectic is likely to prove particularly helpful, because it is in their different assessments of the nature and value of the question and answer debate – in the difference of the postures which they assume on this common ground – that we find the clearest indication of the more general contrast. This is a statement of philosophical method, but it is one which Aristotle would endorse; time and again Aristotle prefers to use, albeit with the refinement which only his own analysis can provide, a current philosophical term or expression rather than a technical term of his own coinage, since by this means he can show how his own analyses and ideas grew out of the general body of ideas already in currency.[66] In *Met.* M4 Aristotle uses the notion of dialectic in this pivotal way to show how first the Socratic interest in definition and then, as a consequence of it, the Platonic hypostatisation of the objects of definition arose from an imperfect appreciation of the nature of dialectic.

Ross comments as follows on Aristotle's remark that in Socrates' time dialectic was not sufficiently developed to study contraries (*ta enantia*) apart from the definition (*ti esti*) – 'Aristotle means that the procedure of which we have an instance in the *Parmenides* . . .

---

[65] See J. M. Le *Blond, Eulogos et L'Argument de Convenance chez Aristote.* The uses of *eulogos* which he distinguishes as '*emploi à défaut d'une certitude*', '*emploi dialectique*' and '*emploi pratique*' all share the feature of indicating that the reasons for saying something are not absolutely conclusive.

[66] Aristotle generally follows the sound advice which he gives at *Top.* B2, 110a16–19, 'one should follow the masses in the nomenclature which one uses for things, but one should not follow them over what sorts of things are and what are not of the kind in question'. For an application of this advice to the analysis of Justice, see J. R. Bambrough, *New Essays on Plato and Aristotle*, pp. 166–7.

where the consequence of contrary hypotheses, "if one is", "if many are", are studied without any definition of one or many having been agreed upon, was not yet a well-recognised mode of discussion in Socrates' time as it afterwards became'.[67] There are a number of objections to this interpretation. Firstly the procedure followed in the *Parmenides* is markedly similar to the method of argument which Zeno apparently practised, that of drawing contrary conclusions from a single hypothesis the meaning of which he confessedly did not understand.[68] Zeno's practice, on this interpretation of it, fits Aristotle's comment at 1078b25–6 as well as does the procedure of the *Parmenides*, if we construe the comment in the way in which Ross does. Since Zeno's practice was available in Socrates' time, Ross's interpretation requires Aristotle's comment to be false. Secondly, although this interpretation may seem to derive support from Parmenides' comment at *Parmenides* 135c8–135d1 that Socrates should undergo training before he attempts 'to mark off (*horizesthai*) a Beautiful and Just and Good and each one of the Forms', a comment which seems to be an injunction against always putting definition first, nevertheless there is some reason to believe that '*horizesthai*' here does not simply mean 'define' in the sense of marking essential rather than non-essential attributes, which is the contrast which Aristotle intends in *Met.* M4. This comment looks like an echo of such passages as *Phaedo* 65d and *Republic* 475e–476a, where Plato is concerned to emphasise the distinctness of each Form from the others rather than to define them. In view of this, I should prefer to translate '*horizesthai*' here by 'distinguish' rather than 'define'.[69] It seems, then, that it is wrong to see an allusion to the procedure of the *Parmenides* in Aristotle's comment at 1078b25–6. It is very probable that the dialectical exercise in the *Parmenides* had a considerable influence on Aristotle when he came to devise his own theory of dialectic, as G. Ryle has recently argued.[70] For in the *Parmenides* we find reasoning which purposely lacks any established ontological basis[71] and uses those common concepts which Aristotle calls the attributes of Being *qua* being –

[67] *Metaphysics*, vol. II, p. 422, *ad* 1078b25.
[68] For Zeno's method, cf. W. K. C. Guthrie, *A History of Greek Philosophy*, vol. 2, p. 82, and the reports of Diogenes Laertius and Sextus Empiricus that in his *Sophistes* Aristotle called Zeno the inventor of dialectic (*Sophistes* fr. 1, Ross, *Aristotelis Fragmenta Selecta*, p. 15); and for his attitude to the hypothesis, cf. the report in Simplicius, *In Phys.* 97.12, 99.13, that according to Eudemus Zeno claimed that he did not understand what a plurality (of units) was because he did not understand what a unit was.
[69] W. G. Runciman, 'Plato's *Parmenides*', pp. 113–15, also notes the difficulty in translating '*horizesthai*' here by 'define'. See also R. Robinson, *Plato's Earlier Dialectic*, pp. 54–5.
[70] *Plato's Progress*, pp. 109, 140–2. [71] 136b7–8.

same, other etc.; and so we find a form of reasoning which conforms closely to Aristotle's description of dialectic in *Met.* Γ2. On the other hand, no special emphasis is placed in the *Parmenides* on these features of the exercise; and it would be fair to say that this work contains a practical example, but no theoretical justification of the practice, of what is developed by Aristotle as the *theory* of dialectic.

There is a further objection to Ross's interpretation of 1078b25–6, the force of which is strengthened if we read the passage uninfluenced by the *Parmenides*. When Aristotle speaks of what can be studied by dialectic independently of definitions – which I have translated 'contraries' (line 26) – it is natural to understand this as 'contrary things' or 'contrary predicates', not 'contrary propositions'. In the great majority of its occurrences the word *enantios* designates the former;[72] and Aristotle has a different and more specialised vocabulary to describe the contrariety of propositions.[73] Where *enantios* is used of the latter, the language in the context usually makes it clear that it is this sort of contrariety which is being considered. An argument in the *De Interpretatione* is particularly revealing.[74] Here Aristotle maintains that it is a mistake to regard beliefs or propositions as contrary just because they are about contrary things: 'the good is good' and 'the bad is bad' are about contrary things but are not themselves contrary propositions. In presenting this argument he uses 'contrary *(enantios)*' by itself to designate contrary things:[75] where contrariety of belief or proposition is being considered, this is clearly signalled by the language of the argument.[76] A further indication that in the *Metaphysics* passage Aristotle is not thinking of contrary propositions is supplied by the next clause – 'and whether the study of contraries is the same' – where he is clearly thinking of contrary things. Since only one of two contrary propositions can be true, only one can be an object of study and knowledge.[77]

[72] cf. Bonitz, *Index*, 246b21–247b38. Only 247a21–31 give examples of contrary propositions, 10 lines out of 141.

[73] *Kataphasis, apophasis, antiphasis*: this type of opposition is distinguished from that of *enantiotēs* in *Cat.* 10, *Top.* B8.

[74] *De Int.* 14, 23a27–23b7.

[75] 23b4, 6.

[76] The remarks about 'the belief *of the contrary*' in 23a34 and 36 might seem to provide an exception to this. But the argument requires that 'the contrary' here designates not the proposition – 'every man is unjust' – but the predicate 'unjust'. Were this not so, Aristotle would be begging the question under consideration, which is precisely whether such a proposition or belief *is* the contrary of 'every man is just'.

[77] cf. also the comparison with sensation in respect of their both being 'of contraries' at *Top.* A10, 104a15, Θ1, 156b11. Sensation has things, not propositions, as its objects.

It would be wrong to overstress this point. There are some passages where Aristotle shows little concern to distinguish contrary things from contrary propositions. Thus in *Rhet.* A1, 1355a19–38, in the course of a comparison between rhetoric and dialectic, it is said that both are concerned to reason towards contrary conclusions (*ta enantia*) and that, despite this, in both types of exercise there is a natural bias towards what is true and right. Here we have an assimilation between the two forms of contrariety; and at later stages of the present argument I shall note further areas where the distinction is blurred.[78] But the point which I want to insist on here is that it is unnatural to construe, with Ross, the mention of 'contraries' in 1078b26 as specifically referring to contrary propositions.

It is clear that if Aristotle should be understood as speaking about contrary *things* at this point, the distinction which he draws here between the study of the definition (*ti esti*) and of contraries is closely related to that which we have already found him drawing in his comments on dialectic in *Met.* B and Γ. Although contrariety is only one of the concepts with which the dialectician is said in *Met.* B1 to be concerned, at *Met.* Γ2, 1004a1–2, and K3, 1061a-10–15, and 1061b4–6, we find the attributes of being *qua* being described generally as 'contraries' or 'contrarieties of what is'. So we should be justified in seeing in the 'contraries' at *Met.* M4, 1078b26, a reference to all the concepts which are said in *Met.* B–Γ to be objects of the dialectician's concern. We saw that in *Met.* B and Γ Aristotle resolves a dilemma about the relationship between dialectic and ontology by distinguishing two ways in which the common attributes of beings can be treated – either as attributes of *beings*, which is the way in which ontology treats them, or simply as general attributes without regard to that of which they are essentially attributes, which is the way in which dialectic treats them. This solution confronts the dilemma, as it was developed in B2, rather obliquely; for the dilemma is developed in terms of the contrast between definition (*ti esti*) and attributes, whereas it is the contrast between *ousia* and attributes which provides the tools for the solution in Γ2. I have already argued[79] that Aristotle's solution is not as oblique as it first appears; for part of the meaning of the word '*ousia*' is 'reality' and in this sense the notions of *ousia* and *ti esti* – i.e. the real nature of the subject, which is aimed at in definition – are connected, while the other part of the meaning of '*ousia*', that of 'substance', is invoked to show that ontology has a central subject-matter with a definite nature of its own. The importance of the remarks on dialectic in *Met.* A6 and M4, and

[78] See p. 30; but for reinforcement of the present point, see pp. 40–1.
[79] pp. 16–17 above.

especially the latter, is that they show how an undeveloped notion of dialectic, which regarded the search for definition as essential to the practice of dialectic, gave rise, in the Platonic developments of ontological theory which grew from reflection on Socratic practice in argument, to what Aristotle believed to be the false ontology of the Forms. In all probability it was this example of the damage to a science (that of ontology) which can result when the nature of the question and answer debate is mistaken, which led Aristotle to require that the connections between dialectic and the scientific notions of *ousia* and *ti esti* be severed. For Aristotle conceived the value of dialectic as essentially residing in its *prescientific* nature, in its ability to debate any particular thesis without the constriction which adherence to any given doctrine would inevitably impose. The comment in *Met.* M4 that in dialectic the study of contraries is not inseparable from the study of definitions makes more intelligible the characterisation in K3 (1061b9) of dialectic as the study of attributes of beings but not *qua* attributes of beings: such a study does not require that those who practise it should adopt any particular attitude towards reality. The recognition that dialectic is not bound to concern itself with definitions is an essential preliminary to the analysis of Γ2 which shows that awareness of the priority of *ousia*, the concept which Aristotle develops in Γ2 to outflank the dilemma of B2 on definition, is not essential for dialectic as it is for ontology.

The addition of the words 'and whether the study of contraries is the same' is puzzling, since it appears that in them we have a specific example of a dialectical proposition[80] placed coordinate with general remarks on dialectic. Accordingly Maier[81] athetised it, and although Ross[82] retained it, he offered no explanation of its place in the argument. The proposition appears frequently in the *Topics* and elsewhere as an example of a dialectical proposition;[83] and it is on occasion positively endorsed by Aristotle as an *endoxon* on which to base an argument.[84] However, there are two considerations which make its mention in *Met.* M4 more reasonable than at first sight appears. Firstly, the proposition that the study of contraries is the same is given in *Top.* A14, 105b23–4, as an example of a 'logical' proposition. This is one of the three sorts of proposition with which dialectic operates. But while the other two sorts, the ethical and physical, also fall within the scope of other forms of intellectual activity than dialectic, there is no study within Aristotle's scheme

[80] cf. *Top.* A14, 105b23–4.
[81] *Die Syllogistik des Aristoteles* II 2, p. 168 n. 4.
[82] *Metaphysics*, vol. 2, p. 422.
[83] cf. Bonitz, *Index* 246a13–18.
[84] e.g. *EN* E1, 1129a13; *De An.* Γ3, 427b5.

which treats such propositions as the one given here as an example of a logical proposition. Accordingly, commentators have accepted Waitz' argument[85] that we should see a reference to dialectic when Aristotle uses the word 'logical (*logikos*)'.[86] 'Logical' propositions fall exclusively within the province of dialectic.[87] Secondly, the origin of the view that the study of contraries is the same is very probably the argument in the *Hippias Minor* that the expert is the man who is most able to produce both the right and the wrong answer.[88] Although Aristotle strongly contests the argument of the *Hippias Minor* that this thesis applies to the case of moral expertise,[89] his frequent use of it in other contexts, where it is not open to the same objections, indicates the considerable influence which it had on him. This *endoxon*, then, is one that typically falls within the province of dialectic and is also clearly associated with Socrates; and so it becomes more understandable that Aristotle should mention it when commenting on the relationship between Socrates' method of argument and his own notion of dialectic. When Aristotle discusses in *Met.* B and Γ the relationship between dialectic and ontology, he mentions not only the contraries themselves (same, other, etc.) but also their attributes, by which he clearly means theses about them. In B1, he asks whose task it is to investigate not only the nature of each of the dialectician's objects but also whether each thing has one contrary, i.e. the *per se* attributes of these objects;[90] and in Γ2 he replies that it falls to the ontologist to examine not only the nature of each of these objects but also their attributes, e.g. whether each thing has one contrary.[91] The fact that there is a mention also in *Met.* M4 of a particular thesis about the dialectician's objects (a thesis which, I have argued, there is good reason to mention in the argument of that passage) confirms my argument[92] that there is a close connection between what Aristotle says about dialectic in M4 and what he says in B2 and Γ2, where there is also a mention of such particular theses.

[85] *Organon*, vol. 2, pp. 353–5.

[86] cf. Ross, *Physics*, p. 540, *ad* 202a21; G. E. L. Owen, 'Logic and metaphysics in some earlier works of Aristotle', p. 167 n. 3.

[87] cf. also *An. Post.* A7, 75b12–14, which gives the proposition that the study of contraries is the same as an example of the sort of general proposition which cannot be treated by any of the special sciences. *An. Post.* A11, 77a26–35, associates such general propositions with dialectic.

[88] 366c–369a; cf. also *Rep.* 333e–334a.

[89] On this, see N. Gulley, *The Philosophy of Socrates*, pp. 136–7. Gulley ignores the attack on the thesis in *Met.* Δ29, 1025a1–13, where Aristotle uses the distinction, vital to his conception of the distinctive character of moral knowledge, between the senses of 'false' in which a man may be said to be false and in which a thing or a statement may be said to be false.

[90] 995b25–7.   [91] 1004b1–8.   [92] pp. 28–9 above.

The Organon on dialectic and the foundations of the sciences

The passages which we have examined in the *Metaphysics* tell a clear and consistent story. They show the distinction between Aristotle's concept of dialectic and that of his predecessors, as well as indicating his notion of its importance in the theory of the forms of intellectual activity. It is now necessary to examine other works, in particular the *Organon*, to see whether they present a picture of the role of dialectic which conforms with that in the *Metaphysics*. This question has assumed greater importance since G. E. L. Owen's justly influential article 'Logic and metaphysics in some earlier works of Aristotle', where it is argued that Aristotle develops in *Metaphysics* Γ, E, Z a concept of a universal science of ontology which is missing from some of his other works and in particular from the *Organon*.[93]

The *Topics* says very little which bears explicitly on the relation between dialectic and other activities. The most important passage is A2, 101a34–b4. The whole chapter discusses the variety of ways in which a work on dialectic can be useful,[94] one of which is 'in relation to the philosophical sciences'. This is explained in 101a34–6, where Aristotle says that ability to argue both sides of a case will increase the ease with which we can sift the truth from what is false. In 101a36–b4 he goes on to argue that dialectic enables us to examine the foundations (*archai*) of each science; this cannot be done by the science itself since it must always reason *from*, and not *to*, its own foundations. When Aristotle begins this argument with the words 'a further use is in relation to the primary items in each science', it looks as if a new use for dialectic is being introduced. Indeed on the surface it appears that different points are made under the headings of 'the philosophical sciences' and 'the primary items in each science'. However, the fact that no such distinction is indicated in the preliminary account of the uses in 101a26–8 should put us on guard against this interpretation, and it is clear from what Aristotle says and practises elsewhere that in 101a34–101b4 he is making a single point. Arguing both sides of the case is a practice which forms the prelude to many of Aristotle's discussions throughout the *corpus* of his works; perhaps the most thorough example is *Met.* B,[95] but it is a constant feature of his

---

93 cf. p. 176: 'But no such science is in view in the *Organon*'. The point is repeated in his *The Platonism of Aristotle*, p. 146: 'Dialectic is quietly demoted to one department of its old province so as to leave room for the new giant' (viz. ontology).

94 101a25–6.

95 cf. B1, 995a24–995b4; the debate is a necessary preliminary to the securing of a proper understanding of the subject.

method and is used in all contexts. The important point is that this debating of the difficulties generally precedes the discussion of the most fundamental concepts which are used in the work in question rather than the discussion of the less important concepts, and so it is fair to say that it is used to treat the foundations rather than what is built upon them. This is one indication of the connection between lines 34–6 and 36 ff. A second is that it is in its use of views (*endoxa*) and of the method of question and answer that dialectic is distinguished from the particular sciences, which are didactic rather than interrogatory and take their start not from views but from premisses which are true and primary;[96] and it is just this feature of dialectic which makes it able to debate *both* sides of the case, regardless of which, if either, is the correct side.[97] So once again[98] we find running through the whole passage 101a34–b4 the closely connected notions of debating both sides of the case,[99] arguing from *endoxic* views,[100] and being critical[101] rather than didactic.

What Aristotle says here about the value of dialectic in investigating the foundations of the sciences is confirmed by what he says in *An. Pr.* A30. This chapter comments briefly on the means of securing a plentiful supply of premisses, which is the precondition of being able to produce demonstrations.[102] Although Aristotle's advice here is very brief and abstract, he refers us for a precise account to the work on dialectic.[103] Ross comments[104] that the reference is to the *Topics* and particularly to A14. However, while it is true that *Top.* A14 discusses the selection of premisses, the discussion is extremely brief and could hardly be called 'a precise working through' of the question.[105] Ross further comments: 'It is, of course, only the selection of the premisses of *dialectical* reasoning that is discussed in the *Topics*; the nature of the premisses of scientific reasoning is discussed in the *Posterior Analytics*'. But Aristotle does not make any such restriction in 46a28–30; rather, the reference to the work on dialectic is clearly intended to cover the selection of *both* types of premiss mentioned in *An. Pr.* A30, those of dialectical and those of apodeictic syllogisms.[106] As for the *Posterior Analytics*, it is not the *nature* of the premisses of scientific reasoning which is at issue in *An. Pr.* A30 but the means of their discovery. On this latter question *An. Post.* is silent except in B19, where Aristotle discusses the means by which we reach awareness of the foundations

---

[96] *Top.* A1, 100a27–100b22; *SE* 2, 165b1–4.
[97] *SE* 11, 172a15–21; dialectic can work with any proposition or its negation but in the demonstrative sciences such licence would spell anarchy, therefore one can proceed by question and answer in dialectic but not in the demonstrative sciences.

[98] cf. p. 29 above. [99] 101a35. [100] 101b1.
[101] 101b3. [102] 46a17–27. [103] 46a28–30.
[104] *Analytics*, p. 396. [105] *An. Pr.* 46a29. [106] cf. 46a8–10.

of the sciences and the character of the awareness which we can have of them.[107] There is no mention of dialectic in this chapter, and it is perhaps this which inclines Ross to restrict the scope of Aristotle's remarks in *An. Pr.* A30, 46a28–30. Nevertheless, this apparent discrepancy can be accounted for by the difference of interest between *An. Post.* B19 and *An. Pr.* A30. In *An. Post.* B19 Aristotle is concerned with the nature of the faculty which apprehends the first principles of the sciences, and with the relation between this faculty and other cognitive faculties which stimulate it to activity. He argues that the first principles are apprehended by intuitive reason (*nous*) and that the faculty which enables us to start on the road to the apprehension of them is sensation;[108] and he traces out the steps (viz. memory and experience) by which the passage from the use of the one faculty to that of the other is effected. In all this the main emphasis is on the psychological question of how the cognitive apparatus which every individual possesses can be developed to the point at which the rare and privileged apprehension of the first principles can be obtained.[109] On the other hand, while *An. Pr.* A30 shares many of the ideas of *An. Post.* B19,[110] it goes beyond *An. Post.* B19 in recognising that there are techniques for organising the *data* of experience into such a form that they can be used as starting-points in demonstration. These techniques are examined in the work on dialectic;[111] and by alluding to them, *An. Pr.* A30 supplements the psychological discussion of *An. Post.* B19 by mentioning the sort of logical procedure which must be employed if we are to harness our cognitive faculties to the task of discovering the first principles. There is no reason to restrict the reference in *An. Pr.* A30 to the single chapter (*Top.* A14) in which Aristotle explicitly comments on the selection of premisses. Aristotle says at *Top.* A13, 105a25–6, that it is possible to reduce three of the four tools (*organa*) which supply us with syllogisms – viz. the detection of ambiguity, the discovery of differences, and consideration of similarities – to the fourth, the securing of premisses; each of these three lines of enquiry will provide us with starting points for reasoning. Since these four tools form the subject matter of *Top.* A13–18 and considerations of ambiguity, similarity, and difference play a large part in the topics which follow in *Top.* B–H, there is no reason to restrict the reference in *An. Pr.* A30 to the single chapter of the *Topics*.

---

[107] 99b17–19.

[108] 100a3–13, 100b13–16.

[109] 99b22–30.

[110] e.g. that experience (*empeiria*) is necessary for the apprehension of the first principles; 46a17–22, cf. 100a4–9.

[111] 46a28–30.

There are several passages in *Top.* Θ where a connection between dialectic and philosophy is indicated. At *Top.* Θ1, 155b1–16, Aristotle says that finding the right topic from which to attack the opposing thesis is a concern shared by both the dialectician and the philosopher, but that arranging the tactics of the questioning is of concern only to the dialectician; the philosopher is not interested in securing the agreement of his opponent. *Top.* Θ14, 163b4–16, recommends that the dialectician should have a variety of arguments against each thesis. Among other benefits, this is of value in philosophical enquiry, where it is important to be able to see the consequences of alternative hypotheses. Another passage in the same vein is *SE* 16, 175a5–12, which mentions two ways in which ability to answer well in debating contests is useful to the philosopher – because it develops in him a sense of the dangers of ambiguity, and because practice in avoiding fallacious reasoning at the hands of others makes it the less likely that he will succumb to it in his private deliberations. It would be wrong to understand the term 'philosophy' in these passages as bearing the hardened sense of *Met.* B–Γ, where it designates an activity which is *both* scientific *and* universal in scope. There are numerous passages in Aristotle's works where the term means no more than positive intellectual enquiry.[112] The passages in the *Topics* and *SE* indicate that dialectic does have power to assist us in disciplines which positively pursue the truth, in spite of the fact that dialectic is essentially neutral with regard to the truth in any matter and is concerned rather to test the merits of both sides of a case without finally pronouncing on which side has the greater merit. Among the disciplines which do positively pursue the truth is the universal science which is called 'philosophy' in the *Metaphysics*.

But rather more important than these passages, which do not give any very substantial information on the part which dialectic can play in scientific enquiry, is *Top.* Θ3, 158a31–158b4. This is the opening section of a chapter in which Aristotle provides hints on how to attack certain theses which do not easily admit of attack. Throughout the chapter there is considerable emphasis on the importance of obtaining definitions from one's opponent in order to facilitate the attack on his thesis.[113] At 158b1–4 and 158b35–159a2 there is special stress on the importance of obtaining definitions when one is faced with a thesis which deals with what is primary and fundamental. It is clear particularly from 158a36–7, 'for it is impossible to *demonstrate* something if one does not start from the *special foundations* and link one's reasoning in a chain until one

---

[112] Some references are given in Bonitz, *Index* 821a8–20.
[113] 158a37–158b4, 17, 21, 158b24–159a2.

THE ORGANON ON DIALECTIC

reaches what is at the end',[114] that in this chapter Aristotle is conscious of the same ideal of scientific reasoning as that which lies behind his remarks in *Top.* A2, 101a34–101b4. This ideal is that expounded in the *Posterior Analytics*, according to which each discrete science has its fundamental elements which must be assumed as a condition of the science and cannot be proved by the science. In *Top.* Θ3 Aristotle regards the examination of these fundamental elements as falling within the scope of dialectic, albeit as one of its more difficult tasks; and so what Aristotle says here confirms what he says rather more forcefully in *Top.* A2 about the value of dialectic in examining those parts of the structure of any science – its foundations – which cannot be examined within the discipline of the science itself.

It may be thought that Aristotle's insistence in *Top.* Θ3 on the important part which definition can play in dialectic is inconsistent with what I argued[115] to be his position in the *Metaphysics*, that it is a mark of the distinction between dialectic and ontology that the former is not, as the latter is, concerned with the definition or nature of the subjects which it treats. This objection could be strengthened by appealing to the fact that one of the forms of proposition which dialectic has to consider is that which states a definition,[116] and that the whole of *Top.* Z and much of *Top.* H is devoted to advising the dialectician on how to deal with definitions. Nevertheless, this objection fails for two reasons. Firstly, propositions which state definitions are only *one* of the four forms of proposition which the dialectician treats; and all that is said in the *Metaphysics* is that the dialectician, by contrast with the ontologist, *need not* put definition first if he is to pursue his activity properly.[117] Secondly, and rather more important, the dialectician works not on *the* definition but on definitions. In *Top.* Θ2, 158a14–21, questions of the form 'what is a man?' are not allowed a place in dialectic, on the grounds that they do not admit of the answer 'yes' or 'no'. To be admissible as dialectical such questions must be put in the form 'is biped footed animal the definition of a man?'.[118] It is, then, the testing of particular proposed definitions, and not the search for

---

[114] These remarks are integral to the argument of this section of the text, since they support the claim in 158a35–6 that proofs about things which are essentially furthest from the foundations are sophistic in character unless they start from what is fundamental and work through all the intermediate steps until the least fundamental is reached; they cannot be regarded as a later insertion into the text.

[115] pp. 25, 29 above.

[116] *Top.* A4, 101b19–25.

[117] cf. *Met.* M4, 1078b25–6, 'dialectic was not yet...capable of *also* examining contraries apart from the definition'; K3, 1061b7–10.

[118] *Top.* A4, 101b26–34.

the definition, which constitutes the dialectician's interest in definition. It is certainly true that *the* definition must be capable of being
actually proposed by some particular person and cannot be known
to be the definition until it has been so proposed and has passed
the sorts of test which are prescribed in the *Topics*. But there remains
an essential difference between the activity which works from actual
examples of definitions and is thereby restricted in its examination
of the definition of the subject to the examples of definitions
actually current, dialectic, and the activity which is not so restricted
but is free to consider any possible definition with a view to securing
the definition, ontology. If we imagine a situation in scholarship in
which the commentator were restricted to the examination of only
the *existing* interpretations of a passage, or even were allowed to
add further interpretations of his own devising, but were prohibited
from choosing from among these interpretations the correct interpretation, we have an analogy with the limited powers of dialectic
in the treatment of definition. Again, there is a similarity between
the distinction between dialectic and ontology which I am here
arguing for and the distinction which is developed in *EN* Γ2–3
between deliberation and choice; without the deliberation and the
reasons for action which it provides there can be no choice of action,
but nonetheless the choice is something distinct from the deliberation
which is its precondition. Similarly, the testing of proposed definitions, which is the task of dialectic, provides reasons for choosing
the definition, but the act of choosing is something distinct from
the testing which necessarily precedes it. This is not to deny the
value of the dialectical treatment of definition. The requirement
that discussion of definitions should proceed in terms of questions
with 'yes' or 'no' answers imposes a discipline which may well be
lacking from the inevitably more open-ended discussion of questions
of the form 'what is X?'. This is a feature of the dialectical exercise
which goes back to Socrates.[119] J. R. Bambrough has rightly emphasised the dangers of expecting that a border-line question, as are so
many of the questions which occupy philosophers, can have a simple
'yes' or 'no' as its answer,[120] and John Wisdom has noted the
important use of the 'what is X?' question by someone who is 'on
the point of modifying an old concept, of developing a related but
new concept'.[121] But an important preliminary to the philosophical

---

[119] cf. Plato *Protagoras* 334c–335a, where Socrates declares his dislike of the
sort of long answer which Protagoras had given in 334a–334c, and his
preference for the short answers, most of them simply 'yes' or 'no', which
Protagoras had given in 332–3.

[120] 'Unanswerable Questions', p. 160.

[121] 'Tolerance', in *Paradox and Discovery*, p. 145. Although Wisdom does
not mention Aristotle here, his remarks fit Aristotle very aptly; cf. e.g.
his procedure in the *De Anima*, where he starts by asking what the soul

examinations of which Bambrough and Wisdom speak is to determine that the question is *not* one to which a simple 'yes' or 'no' answer can be given or that it *is* necessary to modify the old concept; and these points are best determined by the dialectical procedure which works with the current concepts and requires 'yes' or 'no' answers to questions about them.

One noteworthy feature of the passages which I have been discussing is that they are all concerned to emphasise the similarity, rather than the distinction, between dialectic and philosophy. Yet, as we have seen, it is a matter of fundamental disagreement between Plato and Aristotle that there is this distinction. For Plato, the dialectician and the philosopher are identical,[122] whereas Aristotle, in the *Topics* no less than in the *Metaphysics*, rejects this identification. But it is in the *Metaphysics*, rather than in the *Topics*, that the distinction is emphasised. If, as has been often asserted, the *Topics* is an early work, we would expect Aristotle to be more vociferous in his opposition to Plato than in his agreement with him, and thus to place more emphasis on the distinction between dialectic and philosophy. For it is generally when one's awareness of some defect in the work of predecessors is most recent that one most openly and insistently shows hostility towards that work; and although they have not made explicit appeal to this criterion, it is nevertheless notable that many accounts of Aristotle's development have assigned the earlier date to those works which are more critical of Plato and the later to those which are less hostile in tone.[123] If, then, we can accept this criterion for ordering the works – a criterion the value of which is confirmed, although not stated, by the results of those who have investigated problems of ordering – it follows that the lack of emphasis in the *Topics* on the distinction between dialectic and philosophy suggests that the work should not be regarded, as it so often is, as one of Aristotle's earliest works. This is, no doubt, a rather subjective consideration; and I place no great emphasis on it, since my concern is not with questions of the relative chronology of Aristotle's works. But it should be mentioned as a counter to the opposite assumption, that similarities between

is (A1, 402a23–7), examines the views of others on the question (A2–5), and returns to ask the original question and give his own revolutionary answer in B1–3.

[122] *Soph.* 253c–253e.

[123] e.g. the *Eudemian Ethics*, which allows less sense to the claim that there can be a general study of the Good, is dated earlier than the *Nicomachean*, which is not so hostile to this claim; W. K. C. Guthrie in 'The Development of Aristotle's Theology' argues that the *De Caelo*, which in the main explains the motion of the universe in terms solely of the natural motions of its components, is earlier than *Met.* Λ, where we find a reversion to the Platonic idea that the motion of the natural world is to be explained by some first cause which transcends nature.

Academic doctrines and those which are found in the *Topics* indicate an early date for the *Topics*.[124]

The texts which I have examined are in agreement with the account of dialectic which is given in the *Metaphysics*, in two ways: (1) in not limiting the scope of dialectic to any particular department of reality,[125] (2) in making plausible views (*endoxa*) the starting-point in dialectic.[126] But we also saw that a cardinal feature of the account of dialectic in the *Metaphysics* was the view that there are certain things – same, other etc. – with which the dialectician is characteristically concerned; and this is a feature which receives no special emphasis in the descriptions of dialectic, in its relation to philosophy, in the *Topics*.

In fact, the concepts which are mentioned at *Met.* B1, 995b21–2, are all prominent in the *Topics*. Questions about whether two things are the same or other are said to fall under the same heading as questions about definition[127] and are treated in *Top.* H1–2; and in *Top.* A7 we are given an analysis of the senses of 'same'. The notions of similarity and contrariety provide topics in the discussions of accident, genus, property, and definition.[128] The investigation of similarities is also mentioned as one of the tools for securing premisses;[129] and if we may accept the identification of Dissimilarity and Difference, then investigation of dissimilarities is also to be included among the tools.[130] Priority and Posteriority play an

---

[124] Hambruch's essay, *Logische Regeln der platonischen Schule in der aristotelischen Topik*, has been very influential in this direction. Although Hambruch did suppose that his work supported an early dating (p. 32), his main thesis was that the *Topics* is particularly valuable for the interpretation of Academic logical theories. For two recent examples of the inference from similarity of doctrine to an early dating, cf. L. Elders on p. 136 and E. de Strycker on p. 141 of *Aristotle on Dialectic*, ed. G. E. L. Owen.

[125] *Top.* 101b3–4; *Met.* 1004b19–20.

[126] *Top.* 100a30, 101b1; *Met.* 995b24, 1004b25–6.   [127] *Top.* A5, 102a6–10.

[128] Similarity – B10, 114b25–36, 115a15–24; Δ6, 127b26–128a12; E7, 136b33–137a7; E8, 138a30–138b26; H3, 153b36–154a11. Contrariety – B7; B8, 113b27–114a6; Δ3, 123b1–124a9; E6, 135b7–16; Z9, 147a31–147b25; H3, 153a26–153b24.

[129] *Top.* A13, 105a25.

[130] *Top.* 105a24. At *Met.* I3, 1054b23–7, Difference is distinguished from Otherness, which has earlier been assimilated to Dissimilarity (1054b14), on the ground that we must specify the *respect in which* two things are different but need not do this when we say that two things are other. The account of Difference in *Top.* A16 incorporates this point; but at *Top.* Δ4, 125a1–4, where it is also recognised, otherness is nevertheless said to be the genus of difference. In any case, if *Met.* I3 is thought to tell against the identification of Dissimilarity and Difference in the *Topics*, it tells in favour of an identification of Dissimilarity and Otherness, and Otherness, as we have seen, is certainly something which concerns the dialectician.

important part in the discussions of property and definition.[131] So Aristotle's practice in the *Topics* does not belie his general comment in the *Metaphysics* that such general concepts as same, other etc. fall within the province of dialectic.

However, it is also true that no special emphasis is placed in the *Topics* on the use of these concepts in dialectic. We find a practical, rather than a theoretical, demonstration of their importance. For the theory we must turn to the discussions of dialectic in *SE* 9 and 11. In these chapters Aristotle is trying to determine which refutations should be regarded as sophistical and which enquiry is responsible for investigating them. His answer to both questions involves the notion of dialectic. Aristotle distinguishes false refutations which deal with a topic within some particular science and use the premisses peculiar to that science, from those which deal with matters not peculiar to any particular science or deal with matters peculiar to a particular science but do not use the premisses peculiar to the science. Thus a refutation of a thesis about the incommensurability of the diagonal and the side, be it true or false, is nevertheless not a *sophistical* refutation provided that it uses only considerations peculiar to the science in question, in this case geometry.[132] By contrast, an argument which uses Zeno's arguments against the possibility of motion to support an injunction against walking after a meal, although about a medical matter, would not be a medical but rather a sophistical refutation, because it employs considerations which can be applied in a wider area than medicine alone.[133] A further form of sophistical refutation is that which deals with a matter which does not fall under any science at all; in this form of refutation general arguments are used about a general matter (not about a specific matter, as in the other form of sophistical refutation).[134] Since it is a characteristic of dialectic, in contrast to the particular sciences, to lack any special subject-matter, Aristotle can say that only the false refutations which aim at, but fall short of, being dialectical are *sophistical* refutations.[135]

Aristotle rejects the suggestion that there could be any skill which treated *all* false refutations:[136] to admit such polymathy would run

---

[131] E3, 131a12–26; Z4, 142a22–142b19.

[132] *SE* 9, 170a23–34; 11, 171b12–16, 171b37–9. This form of paralogism is also distinguished from the sophistical at *Top.* A1, 101a5–17.

[133] *SE* 11, 172a8–9.

[134] cf. 11, 171b8–12: 'one type of eristic and sophistic reasoning is that which appears to reason on matters where dialectic tests...and *(scil.* the other is) all those cases of false reasoning *(paralogismoi)* which do not conform with the particular line of enquiry but seem to belong to the skill'.

[135] 9, 170a34–9; 11, 171b34–7.

[136] 9, 170a20–4.

quite counter to his notion of specialist and antonomous expertises. Consequently he delimits the class of refutations which can be called sophistical; and he does this by exploiting two aspects of the notion of dialectic. Firstly, dialectic is a skilful activity;[137] and so he is as justified in describing sophistical refutations as deviations from the norm of competent dialectic, as he is in deprecating the poor performance which is represented by *false* (but not sophistical) refutations within any of the special sciences. Secondly, dialectic cannot be ranked simply coordinate with the special sciences, despite the fact that it is like them in being an activity which requires skill, since unlike them it has no special subject-matter.[138] It is for this reason that Aristotle can describe as sophistical the false refutations which apply general considerations to the subject-matter of a special science: the possibility of such refutations arises from the fact that dialectic has no special subject-matter. On the other hand, dialectic is a skill distinct from that in each of the special sciences; so it can be maintained that sophistical refutations, for all their use of general considerations, do constitute a *special* class of refutations. In fact, the two types of sophistical refutations can be assimilated, since the general considerations which are mis-applied to the special sciences in the one type, are just those which are proper to dialectic. Because dialectic is both a skill and of general application, Aristotle is able to use the notion of dialectic to locate a genuine class of sophistical refutations.

So sophistical refutations are those which masquerade as dia-lectical, and it is the task of the dialectician to study them.[139] In his account in *SE* 11 of the contrast between dialectic and the special sciences Aristotle describes the objects with which dialectic is concerned as 'common (*ta koina*)' as opposed to the objects which are special to each of the special sciences.[140] The contrast is amplified as follows:

Now since there are many things which are identical whatever they are predicated of but are not such as to be of a natural kind – rather, they are like negatives – while others are not like this but are specialised, it is possible by means of the former things to conduct examinations in any area and for there to be an art of this – one which is unlike those which give demonstrative proof.[141]

---

[137] 11, 172a34–6.
[138] 9, 170a33–9; 11, 172a11–15, 36–40.
[139] 9, 170b5–11; 11, 172b5–8.
[140] 11, 172a32; cf. *An. Post.* A11, 77a26–35.
[141] 11, 172a36–40. Translators (e.g. Pickard-Cambridge, Forster) tend to read the first two lines as speaking of identical principles rather than things; but their versions are not able to accommodate convincingly the subsequent reference to kinds and negatives.

The particular importance of these remarks lies in their description of the dialectician's 'common objects' as things or predicates and not as propositions: Aristotle regards it as meaningful, although incorrect, to speak of them as 'kinds'. Although the word 'negative (*apophasis*)' is most commonly used to mean the negation of a proposition, on occasion it is used of negative predicates. Thus when Aristotle says that the Platonists did not admit Forms of negatives, he means that they would not recognise such Forms as Not-Man.[142] So in this use of the word, 'negatives' are negations of kinds; and like the kinds they are not propositions but rather things or predicates. I have argued that in the *Metaphysics* Aristotle consistently represents the dialectician's objects as things or predicates.[143] Although it is not said in *SE* 11 what these 'common things' are, there is no reason to suppose that they are not the same as those associated with the dialectician in the *Metaphysics* since, as we have seen, these are all prominent in the *Topics*. So *SE* 11 provides evidence that the doctrine of common dialectical objects is not peculiar to the *Metaphysics* but has its place in the *Organon* also.

Dialectic and the study of everything

An important premiss to Aristotle's argument in *SE* 9 and 11 is that there is no science which investigates everything. At the beginning of chapter 9 he says:

As for the number of factors by which persons are refuted, one should not try to grasp this without a science of everything there is. *But this does not belong to a single skill*; for the sciences are perhaps unlimited in number, so that clearly the demonstrative proofs are too. (170a20–3)

It is the denial that there is a single science of all things which leads Aristotle to restrict the field of refutations which can be called sophistical to those which attempt to employ dialectical techniques.[144] At 172a9–15, in support of his comment that false refutations which relate to the subject-matter of a special science may nevertheless be sophistical refutations, Aristotle notes that the dialectician has no definite subject-matter and goes on, 'for neither is it the case that everything falls within some single kind, nor, if this were the case, could existing things fall under the same foundations'. There seems, then, to be no room in *SE* 9 and 11 for the universal science of ontology which Aristotle argues for in the

---

[142] *Met.* M4, 1079a7–10; for the sense of 'negative (*apophasis*)' here, cf. *Peri Ideōn* fr.3 (Ross, *Fragmenta*, p. 123, = Alexander *In Metaphysica* 80.15–21), where Aristotle exemplifies a negative with the predicate 'not-man'.
[143] pp. 27–8 above.   [144] 170a34–9.

Metaphysics; and since the account of dialectic in the *SE* is in agreement with what is said on the subject in the *Topics*, G. E. L. Owen has argued[145] that the account of dialectic in the *Organon* represents an earlier *stratum* in Aristotle's thought which cannot be incorporated in entirety into the later stage which is represented by *Met.* Γ, E, Z with its account of the universal science. Owen's main thesis is that (1) in the *Metaphysics* the possibility of a universal science depends on the analysis of 'being' which shows it to be, although not univocal, nevertheless not equivocal but rather a word with a primary sense (that of 'substance') and also secondary senses which must be explained in terms of the primary sense, and (2) in certain other works, and also in parts of the *Metaphysics*, Aristotle either shows no awareness of the possibility of this *tertium* between univocity and equivocity or fails to apply it to 'being'. A consequence of failure to apply what Owen calls the concept of focal meaning to the analysis of 'being' will be a denial of the possibility of a universal science, and Owen finds such a denial at *EE* A8, 1217b35, as well as at *SE* 9, 170a20–3, and 11, 172a13–15.

Nevertheless, there are reasons for supposing that the opposition between what Aristotle says in these passages and what he says in *Met.* Γ, E, Z is not as great as Owen thinks. In *Met.* E1 Aristotle contrasts the special sciences with the universal science in that while they study some particular part of what there is, some circumscribed *kind* of thing, the universal science studies what there is quite generally, without any such limitation or qualification.[146] Later in the same chapter he identifies this general ontology with theology, the study of unchanging substance, and rationalises this identification with the remark that the study of unchanging substance is primary and *universal in the sense that it is primary*.[147] Behind this problematic description of ontology lie some difficulties and doctrine which are material to the present question. At *EE* A8, 1218a1–15, Aristotle argues that where we have a series in which one member is prior and others posterior, we cannot allow that all the members share a common characteristic which is distinct from any of them, since that distinct characteristic would then be prior to all the members of the series and thus would claim the primacy which was originally assigned to the primary member. This argument lies behind the comment in *Met.* B3, 999a6–10, that there can be no distinct universal which covers such series as those of numbers or shapes or, generally, any group in which there are prior and posterior members. It is also to be detected in the remark at *EE* H2, 1236a23–5, 'In every case persons seek what is primary, but because the universal is primary they assume that the primary is universal;

145 In 'Logic and Metaphysics in Some Earlier Works of Aristotle'.
146 1025b8–10.   147 1026a29–32.

but this is an error'. This comment comes in Aristotle's analysis of the complexity of the concept of friendship, which Owen argues is a case of focal meaning which the *Eudemian Ethics does* recognise. It is clear that it is derived from the argument of *EE* A8 that the primacy of the universal (an *endoxon* which in these contexts Aristotle allows to stand for the sake of argument *ad hominem*) excludes any claim to primacy which may be made for something which falls under that universal.

In these contexts Aristotle uses these theses polemically to exploit difficulties in rival accounts, such as Plato's,[148] where he feels that the difference between the universal and the paradigm case has not been clearly appreciated. The universal, if it is conceived as covering all the members of the series, cannot be identified with the primary member: for if it were, it would not cover all members of the series to the same degree. Yet only if this identity *does* obtain can the primacy claimed for the universal be reconciled to that claimed for the first member of the series. In other contexts, where Aristotle is not so concerned to exploit difficulties in the Platonic ontology, he shows the same concern for the dangers of confusing the universal and the primary case. At *De An.* B3, 414b20–415a13, Aristotle says that the forms of soul, like the forms of geometrical shapes, constitute a series with prior and posterior members, and that in the case of such series any common definition which might fit all the members would fail to indicate the distinct nature of each of them. Accordingly, instead of looking for a common definition we should try to give an individual definition of each of the members of the series and also to show how they are ordered in the series.[149] He offers a similar analysis of the definition of the citizen at *Pol.* Γ1, 1275a33–1275b21. The kinds of constitution form a series,[150] and so also do the kinds of citizen.[151] So we should not expect that the most satisfactory definition of one of these kinds will also be the one which best fits the others.[152] These comments on the definition of the complex concepts of soul and citizen are a practical application of the arguments about separate universals and series which are found in *EE* A8, H2, and *Met.* B3; and the similarity between the analysis of soul in *De An.* B3 and the analysis of being in *Met.* Γ2 is recognised by Owen.[153] The notion of a series is also prominent in Aristotle's account in the *Metaphysics* of the position of universal ontology in the system of scientific activities. At *Met.* Γ2, 1004a2–9, he says:

---

[148] cf. *Peri Ideōn* fr.4 (Ross, *Fragmenta*, p. 126 = Alexander *In Metaphysica* 85.18–86.10). This matter will be discussed in chapter 3, especially pp. 94–103 below.

[149] 414b32–4. [150] 1275a35–1275b3. [151] 1275b3–5.

[152] 1275a33–8, b5–7. [153] p. 173.

There are as many parts of philosophy as there are substances; so some must be primary and others of them next in order. For Being falls directly into kinds; and so the sciences also will follow these. For the philosopher is like the person named after mathematics; for this too has parts, and there is a primary science and a secondary one and others successively within mathematics.

This idea of a series of sciences lies behind the description in *Met.* E1 of theology as *first* among the studies of substances.[154]

This, then, is the background against which Aristotle's characterisation of theology as 'universal in the sense that it is primary' should be read. Aristotle is not here contradicting his assertion in the *EE* that the primary form in the series does *not*, as a universal *does*, cover all the other forms. He is rather saying that insofar as it is permissible to call the primary form universal, theology can, as the primary form of science, be called universal. But the sort of universality which characterises the primary case is not the sort of universality which is possessed by the attribute which all the cases, primary and otherwise, share. Thus whenever someone has a certain amount of money or possessions, however small, we may speak of *his* wealth, but we can speak of *wealth* only where the amount is sizeable and exceptional. What is common to all the cases of possession is not the characteristic of being wealth but that of being *someone*'s wealth, and so in this sense wealth is not the universal characteristic. On the other hand, what unifies all these dissimilar cases of possession is their approximation to, and in some cases realisation of, the common standard of *wealth*, and without this standard they would not constitute a genuine group which could meaningfully be said to have a universal characteristic; in this sense it is the primary case, the standard, which is universal. In the passages which I have been examining Aristotle's argument is, in

---

[154] Physics is called second philosophy at *Met.* Z11, 1037a15.

It will be seen that I do not accept the argument of Jaeger (*Aristotle*, pp. 216–19) that *Met.* E1 represents a conflation of two views of philosophy – as general ontology and as the study of the highest form of substance – which were originally distinct and which Aristotle has not fully succeeded in welding together. Certainly the objects of theology (*theologikē*), which are primary among substances, are only a sub-class of *all* substances, the primacy of which is appealed to when Aristotle describes his notion of a general ontology; but I believe that it could be shown that not only is philosophy the study of everything in general but of substance in particular, but also, and more definitely, it is the study of substances in general but of unchanging substance in particular. However, this point does not affect the present thesis. What is important is that *Aristotle* felt that the two views of philosophy were not incompatible, and justified this with the expression 'universal in the sense that it is primary'; and this Jaeger does accept (p. 218). See also G. Patzig, 'Theologie und Ontologie in der "Metaphysik" des Aristotles', p. 196.

effect, that certain concepts – Friendship, Soul, Citizen, Shape, Being, Philosophy – have a complexity such that their unity can only be preserved by their possessing some central element to which, like a standard case, reference must be made when we explain how the other elements belong to the same concept. This primary element is universal in the sense in which Wealth is. But Aristotle usually means by 'universal' the common characteristic of a number of instances: this is what he calls the 'one over many' – Man, for example, as opposed to individual men. In this sense the universal is Being Someone's Wealth rather than Wealth. Accordingly in *EE* H2 he distinguishes the primary case from the universal, and in *Met.* E1 he expressly speaks of *the sort of* universality possessed by the primary case.[155]

It is notable that in the passages where Owen detects a failure to apply the notion of focal meaning to the concept of Being, and a consequent failure to appreciate the possibility of a universal science, the argument is directed against the idea that all beings belong to the same genus. This is particularly clear in the argument of *SE* 11, 172a11–15, that dialectic cannot be a science because what falls within its scope, i.e. everything, does not belong to a single genus or fall under the same basic principles.[156] However, the idea that all the things which fall under a complex concept such as that of Being share the same characteristic is, as we have seen, one which Aristotle also resolutely opposes in those passages which *do* show awareness of the possibilities for analysis which the notion of focal meaning provides. Further, in those passages which do seem quite uncompromisingly to deny the possibility of a universal science closer examination of the text makes us hesitate. Thus, at *Met.* A9, 992b18–19, he says: 'The whole enterprise of searching for the elements of things which are cannot be achieved *unless persons make distinctions*, since things are said to "be" in many senses.' Here it is important to note the qualification. It is essential to Aristotle's concept of a universal science that the variety of the senses of 'being' should be appreciated; and the philosopher who attempted to prosecute such a science without giving any account of this variety of senses would be a target for the sort of attack on universal definition which is found at *De An.* B3 and *Pol.* Γ1 and which underlies the account of the nature of universal science in *Met.* Γ and E. Owen's argument can claim most support from *EE* A8, 1217b33–5, where Aristotle argues from the variety of the senses of 'being' to the impossibility of any science of being: this is more

---

155 The nature and importance of this distinction is further discussed in chapter 3, pp. 64–7 below.
156 cf. *An. Post.* B7, 92b13–14: 'Being is not the real nature of anything; for what is is not a genus.'

radical than the argument in *Met.* A9, where what is rejected is the possibility of a science of being which is innocent of this variety of senses. The argument here against the science of being is an offshoot of a more detailed argument against the science of goodness. In this more detailed argument Aristotle charges the philosopher who attempts the general study of goodness not only with the over-simplification involved in ignoring the ambiguities which differences of category import[157] but also with ignoring the difference between types of goodness which fall in the same category.[158] It appears, then, that in *EE* A8 Aristotle delivers a rebuke against those who fail to appreciate the complexity of the subject which they propose to study, of which only one part exploits the ambiguities which the doctrine of categories reveals and which are argued in the *Metaphysics* not to be fatal to the enterprise of a general science of being. The attack is directed against all forms of over-simplification whereby failure to appreciate the complex nature of some subject of study is reflected in failure to appreciate that there are many ways of studying that subject; these studies need to be distinguished and articulated just as much as do the elements in the subject itself.

This brings us to a more general point. I have argued that for Aristotle the concept of philosophy shares the complexity of the concepts of being, soul etc. and is to be analysed in the same way, i.e. as containing a central and primary element which unifies all the other elements in the complex. First philosophy is not the whole of philosophy; and to suppose that studies other than first philosophy cannot be philosophies is to make the mistake of those who do not allow that cases of other forms of friendship than the primary form are cases of friendship at all,[159] or that it is possible to be a citizen under any form of constitution other than the primary form. In fact the other forms of philosophy have their own spheres of operation, and what they say within these spheres is no less true for not being an assertion made by first philosophy. Physics is concerned with its subjects not in respect of their being but in respect of their motion;[160] and although it is true that mathematics assumes certain things to be true of sensible, moving bodies which are not true of them in respect of their being sensible and moving, nevertheless the subjects which mathematics studies are real and what it says about them is true.[161] So we must not misunderstand what Aristotle says about the universality of first philosophy as meaning that there is no room for other forms of philosophy which investigate matters

[157] 1217b26–35.
[158] 1217b35–41.
[159] *EE* H2, 1236a26–30.
[160] *Met.* K3, 1061b6–7, cf. *Met.* M3, 1077b22–7.
[161] *Met.* M3, 1078a28–30.

which do not fall within the province of first philosophy.[162] If we find Aristotle denying that there is any science which studies everything, his denial is to be understood in the context of this analysis of the relation between the forms of philosophy.

Aristotle is careful in the *Metaphysics* to describe first philosophy as the study of that which is *in respect of its being*. This is a universal study, since it is true of everything that it is. But the attribute of Being is not the only attribute which things possess, and the *Metaphysics* argues that the study of these further attributes belongs not to first philosophy but to the other forms of philosophy. On two occasions Aristotle rejects the idea that physics is first philosophy on the grounds that not everything is capable of being moved or producing movement.[163] These passages show Aristotle rejecting the claim of physics to the title of first philosophy on the grounds that physics is not, as first philosophy must be, the study of everything. But the notion of 'the study of everything' needs to be analysed. Aristotle recognises the ambiguity of the word 'thing' as between the subject and its attributes – i.e. the difference in sense when we speak of the *things* that there are and when we speak of the *things* that are true of these things.[164] Aristotle has at hand the conceptual tools for analysing 'the study of everything' as either (1) 'the study of something about everything', or (2) 'the study of everything about something', or (3) 'the study of everything about everything'. I have argued that of these possible interpretations the first represents Aristotle's conception of the universal science, since it is his view that this science studies some particular aspect of everything – viz. their being. By contrast, (2) approximates to Aristotle's conception of a special science which exhaustively studies the attributes of some particular part of reality. But in the *Metaphysics* the limitations of this conception of a special science are repeatedly exploited,[165] and awareness of this limitation is reflected in the characterisation, in

---

[162] cf. *De An.* A1, 403a29–403b16, where there is a discussion of the variety of ways in which the properties of the soul can be investigated. The manner in which first philosophy approaches the matter is only one among many possibilities (403b15–16).

[163] *Met.* E1, 1026a27–30; *PA* A1, 641a34–641b10.

[164] *Met.* Z1, 1028a30–1; *An. Post.* A4, 73b5–8. Both these passages point to a difference in the senses of 'be' according to which subjects and attributes are said to 'be'.

[165] I think here particularly of the frequently expressed difficulties in *Met.* Γ about this conception of a science (cf. pp. 16–17 above), and of the picture of the special sciences which is presented in *Met.* M3 according to which the validity of each of the special sciences depends on their concentrating on some aspect of their subject which is necessarily ignored by the other sciences which treat the same subject. Thus, although arithmetic treats Man as something indivisible and geometry treats him as something divisible, both approaches are correct (1078a21–31).

Met. E1, of these special sciences as other than primary. I have argued that (3) is a misinterpretation of what Aristotle means by the universal science. But it is a misinterpretation which is easily put on the expression 'the study of everything'.[166] I maintain that in rejecting the conception of a 'science of *all* the things that are' in *SE* 9, 170a21, and of a '*single* science of what is' in *EE* A8, 1217b35, Aristotle is rejecting the conception of a universal science which would see it as the study of everything about everything; and I have emphasised the words in the quotations to show how natural it is that in both these passages he should reject a universal science given that in both of them he is anxious to emphasise the variety of the special sciences. For this variety must be appreciated if we are to understand both the privileged position, and the limitations to the privilege of that position, which Aristotle claims for first philosophy among the sciences. I conclude that in those passages where Aristotle rejects the possibility of the study of everything he is rejecting (3) and in those passages where he accepts the possibility of such a study he is accepting (1), and that the difference between the two types of passage is indicated by details of language in them. It seems to me that Owen has not allowed for the difference between (1) and (3) when he argues for an inconsistency between *Met.* Γ, E, Z on the one hand and the *EE* and the *Organon* on the other.

It is natural that Aristotle should consider interpretation (3) in those passages where the possibility of the study of everything is rejected. In both *SE* 9, 11 and *EE* A8 he is concerned with the notion of dialectic, either positively, as in *SE*, where he speaks of his own notion of dialectic, or negatively, as in *EE*, where he wishes to combat a notion of dialectic which is Platonic and false.[167] Dialectic is indeed concerned with everything about everything, as first philosophy is not; but the price which it pays for this universality is that, unlike first philosophy, it is not scientific in character. The universality of dialectic is opposed to the universality of first philosophy in the same way in which, in our example above, the universality of the notion of Wealth is opposed to that of the notion of Someone's Wealth. First philosophy is restricted, in its study of everything, to that characteristic – Being – which everything shares: by contrast, there is no question which is closed to dialectic. Accordingly, although it is true that first philosophy examines those common axioms, such as the principle of non-contradiction, which

---

[166] It is naturally suggested by *P.A.* A1, 641b1, 'so natural philosophy would be concerned with *everything*'.

[167] cf. 1217b20–4, where the positing of Ideas, including that of Good, is characterised as 'logical (*logikōs*)': this means that Aristotle saw the Ideas as arising from the practice of dialectic (see p. 30 above) and, moreover, from the poor practice of it (see pp. 15–16 above).

because of their generality cannot form the subject-matter of any special science but are of concern to the dialectician,[168] it is dialectic alone that can examine the special foundations of each science.[169] This is the value which dialectic uniquely possesses, and it is a value which is not superseded by the different value possessed by first philosophy. However, the sort of universality which characterises dialectic prevents it from being scientific. The wealth possessed by the individuals each of whom has his own wealth may well differ for each individual and can only be described as common to all of them in the sense in which not being a man is common to such different things as horses, tables, numbers etc. Aristotle alludes to this when he says that the subject-matter of dialectic is not of any definite nature but is rather to be compared to negatives.[170] Throughout his works, in the *Organon* and the *Metaphysics* alike, Aristotle presents a consistent picture of the relationship between dialectic and science and of the respective values of each.

Summary: Aristotle and Plato on dialectic and science

I opened this chapter with a comment on the fundamental opposition between Plato and Aristotle on the question of the unity of science, and I suggested that the nature of the opposition between the two philosophers was likely to be most clearly shown in their differing evaluations of the common activity of dialectic. In this chapter I have been concerned not so much with the details of the practice of the question and answer debate, which is most fully discussed in *Top.* Θ, as with the location of dialectic in Aristotle's system of the forms of expertise. This has required an examination of a number of passages, mainly in the *Metaphysics* and the *Organon*, where the relations between dialectic, the special sciences, and the universal science are discussed. I have argued that the notion of substance (*ousia*) which he develops out of the more primitive notion of the nature (*ti esti*) supplies the tool by which in the *Metaphysics* Aristotle is able to distinguish the universal science both from the special sciences and from dialectic. Aristotle uses the notion of substance to break the dilemma of *Met.* B2, which confronted the idea of a universal science with the difficulty that essence (i.e. that aspect of *ousia* in which the word is interchangeable with '*ti esti*') falls outside the scope of scientific proof. He shows that *ousia* in the sense of 'substance' which he himself discovered by analysis, is an essential element in the explanation of anything which is said to be; and thus he vindicates its claim to be the subject-

---

[168] *Met.* Γ3; *An. Post.* A11, 77a26–35.
[169] *Top.* A2, 101a34–101b4; cf, *An. Pr.* A30, discussed pp. 32–3 above.
[170] *SE* 11, 172a36–8.

matter of a science. In the case of dialectic the notion of *ousia* operates less directly. It provides, as I have said, a focus of unity for the concept of being; and this concept in turn constitutes a subject with attributes, and one from which its attributes are notionally isolable. The possibility of this isolation provides Aristotle with his characterisation of dialectic as an activity which is concerned with the characteristics which things possess simply in virtue of being things but not with the being in virtue of which these characteristics are possessed. When he examines Plato's ontology, he uses this conception of dialectic to show that Plato was misled into devising an incorrect ontology by an incorrect notion of dialectic. For Plato conceived dialectic as essentially involving a search for definitions, and he regarded it as a scientific activity. From this it followed that he regarded the objects of the dialectical science – the definitions – as separate entities; and Aristotle would allow this as a reasonable step for Plato to make, since he too regarded the object of the universal science – Substance – as a separate entity.[171] But Aristotle maintains that dialectic does not involve the search for definitions; and in doing this he undermines one of the main props of the theory of Forms.[172]

Aristotle preserves the Platonic idea of dialectic as unrestricted in its scope. On the other hand this lack of restriction is for Aristotle an indication of the unscientific character of dialectic, whereas for Plato it had been an indication that dialectic was the only true science. This opposition between the philosophers derives from Aristotle's analysis of the concept of philosophy as a complex in which the genuinely universal element also has a particular form and only partially covers the other elements. Aristotle is able by means of his category distinction between subject and attribute to unravel the ambiguity in the notion of the study of everything and so to make the distinction, which is lacking to Plato, between ontology, which studies everything *in the respect in which* all things constitute a unity, and dialectic, which does not as an intellectual activity have such a structure as to reflect any unity in the subjects which it treats. To be sure, Plato had attempted with the Form of Good to confer unity on the subjects of his dialectic; but the attempt was bound to founder on objections derived from the complexity of the concept of being, or from (what is simply the same point, cast in the linguistic mode) the ambiguity of the word 'being', in the absence of the sort of analysis which Aristotle provides in *Met.* Γ2.

Nevertheless Plato was correct in his assessment of the need for

---

[171] Not, of course, the universal – Substance – but the instances (substances) which fall under the universal, cf. *Met.* Z3, 1029a28.
[172] *Met.* A6, M4.

such a unifying element; and accordingly, where Aristotle finds such an element in the notion of substance, he makes this the basis of his own universal science. His *dialectic*, on the other hand, follows its Platonic forbear in being completely unrestricted in scope and also in its lack of any unifying element; but Aristotle recognises, as Plato did not, both the absence and the need for the absence of such an element in *dialectic*. For just as dialectic is an activity which *precedes* the special sciences and provides the means of investigating their foundations which they are unable themselves to provide, so also it *precedes* the universal science of ontology; it should not be hampered in its operation by the acceptance of any particular ontological thesis, an acceptance which *is* necessary within the science of ontology as it is within any science.[173] In his own investigations in ontology Aristotle makes dialectic do double service. It provides the means of attacking Plato's ontology. That this is so is clear not only from the many examples in the *Topics* of arguments against the theory of Forms, but also from *EE* A8, 1217b16–19, and *Met.* M5, 1080a9–11, which refer us to another work or department of enquiry for a fuller treatment of the theory of Forms. In both passages the enquiry referred to is described as 'more logical', which is generally accepted by commentators as designating dialectic;[174] and that the reference is indeed to dialectic is made irresistible by the comment in *EE* A8, that this enquiry contains 'arguments which are at the same time both destructive and general'.[175] It also provides him with the means to lay the foundations of his own exercise in ontology: the remarks in *Met.* B1, 995a24–995b4, which introduce the examination of difficulties which is a necessary preliminary to the establishment of the foundations of ontology, indicate clearly that a dialectical exercise is to follow. So in order to preserve the cardinal value of dialectic in this respect, Aristotle must correct Plato and free dialectic from ontology. I have argued that just such an interpretation of the nature of dialectic is to be found in the comments of *Met.* Γ2 and M4 on the independence of dialectic from concern with substance (*ousia*) or the nature (*ti esti*) of things.

A final way in which the superiority of Aristotle's tools of analysis shows itself when the theories of Plato and Aristotle on dialectic are compared, lies in the difference between the manner in which each supposes dialectic to be of value in scientific enquiry. Aristotle regards each science as essentially resting on its own foundations, which are

[173] cf. *SE* 11, 172a15–21.
[174] cf. p. 30 above.
[175] cf. G. E. L. Owen, *The Platonism of Aristotle*, p. 145: 'Aristotle came to think that dialectic itself was competent to undermine the Theory of Forms.'

objectively and universally valid in such a way that it is meaningless to suggest that in addition to these there might be other foundations which are *the* foundations. At the same time, however, he is able, by means of his distinction between that which is more intelligible *absolutely* and that which is more intelligible *to us*, to allow that there are foundations which are other than *the* foundations. For it is the nature of foundations to exceed that of which they are foundations in intelligibility; and so the distinction between the absolute and the relative forms of intelligibility will be reflected in a distinction between absolute and relative forms of foundations. Accordingly, Aristotle can say *both* that dialectic is concerned with the foundations of science,[176] *and* that dialectic and science are essentially opposed, in that the former can never get beyond the method of question and answer while the latter is essentially didactic.[177] Plato lacked the distinction between the two modes of being more intelligible and the corresponding distinction between the two modes of being a foundation. Consequently he regarded it as the job of dialectic to concern itself with both sorts of foundation. Although Plato distinguished in the *Republic* between the passage which leads up to the first principle and that which leads down from it, he regarded it as the function of dialectic to effect both these passages.[178] The distinction between the upward and downward paths had a strong influence on Aristotle's conception of science. But he is also aware of the difficulty involved in assigning the dual role to dialectic which Plato had given it; and he solves the difficulty by means of his distinction between the two forms of intelligibility.[179]

Aristotle regards it as the job of dialectic to proceed from *foundations* to *the* foundations. In science the foundations are first and can only be argued *from*. In dialectic the foundations are argued *to*, from foundations which are not *the* foundations. One of the more important achievements of Aristotle's theory of the forms of intellectual exercise is to disarm the apparent paradox in this.

[176] *Top.* A2, 101a34–101b4; Θ3, 158a31–158b4. For further discussion of this, see pp. 68–73, 89–93 below.

[177] *SE* 2, 165b3; 11, 172a15–21.

[178] *Rep.* 511b; dialectic proceeds 'up to the unhypothetical first principle of everything' and then 'descends to the conclusion'.

[179] At *EN* A4, 1095a32–1095b4, he notes that Plato debated whether investigation should proceed *to* or *from* the foundations. There is no hint that Plato resolved his doubts on this matter. Aristotle's own solution uses the distinction between the two forms of intelligibility.

3

OBJECTS AND FACULTIES

In the previous chapter I supported my analysis of Aristotle's ideas about dialectic by appealing to certain philosophical distinctions. To elucidate Aristotle's remarks about dialectic and definition, I emphasised the distinction between definitions and *the* definition; and I relied on an analogous distinction between foundations and *the* foundations of a science to characterise the role of dialectic in this area. I also argued that an important element in Aristotle's distinction between dialectic and first philosophy is that each possesses a different sort of universality, and that it is essential to appreciate this if we are to assess the contributions which each activity has to make to our understanding of things. Clearly all of these points require closer philosophical scrutiny; and this I shall attempt in the present chapter. At the same time it is important to establish that the analyses in question are of an Aristotelian character, if we are to be justified in using them to elucidate his concept of dialectic. Accordingly I shall examine at length a passage in the *Nicomachean Ethics*. The subject-matter of the passage is not dialectical (although its method is); but I shall argue that it provides a metaphysical theory of very wide application.

The philosophical insights of Wittgenstein, Wisdom and Bambrough have helped me to find this theory in the work of Aristotle. I hope that, once found, it will not continue to elude commentators on Aristotle, as it has done so far. The theory provides analytic support for the theses which were used in chapter two. Moreover it can be applied to the exploration of concepts which are central to dialectic, and it was so applied by Aristotle. So after exploring the general theory, we shall return to a direct examination of Aristotle's concept of dialectic armed with tools which have been further tested.

The object of wish

In his paper 'Mace, Moore, and Wittgenstein'[1] Wisdom, developing a point from Mace, gives a brief but extremely suggestive analysis of the statement 'It's amusing' and of the conditions which surround

[1] *Paradox and Discovery* (Oxford, 1965), pp. 148–66.

the upholding or challenging of a claim that something is amusing.[2] He notes that the question of whether something is amusing is not the same as a question about one's own feelings of amusement, nor again the same as a question about the reactions of amusement in the audience at large. To report one's own feelings or the general reaction of the audience is not sufficient if one wishes to decide whether something is amusing. On the other hand (and here I go beyond what Wisdom says in this place)[3] a question about whether something is amusing is essentially a question about feelings and reactions of amusement. It is not the case that the feelings and reactions of amusement are irrelevant to the settling of the question; rather, there is nothing more to use in settling the question than the feelings and reactions of oneself and the rest of the audience and other people who, though not present at the event, could be imagined to be so. I do not mean by this to restore to the question the subjectivity which Wisdom hoped to remove. The effect of Wisdom's observations is to show that in addition to observing people's feelings, one needs *reasons* if one is to support the claim that something is amusing. Nevertheless, the reasons are reasons for being amused and to be amused is to feel amused. So the question *is* about people's feelings of amusement, but not about the feelings of any particular person or group of people at any particular time. If we allow that there is a right answer to the question, we may say that it is about the feelings of the expert in these matters, provided that we recognise that being an expert is defined by the ability regularly to get the right answer to such questions. But there is value in introducing the notion of the expert here. For it serves as a corrective to the plausible but wrong accounts of the nature of the question. Such wrong accounts are those which reduce the question whether something is amusing to (a) 'It makes me laugh', or (b) 'It makes the majority laugh', or again (c) 'It seems amusing to me', or (d) 'It seems amusing to the majority', or again (e) 'It has certain qualities which make it amusing even though it may never provoke any laughter or feelings of amusement in anyone'.

All these reductions illuminate certain aspects of the matter at the expense of obscuring others. They are distinct reductions, each apparently opposed to the others; and since between them they seem to represent all the possible interpretations of what it is to be amusing, there is the temptation, which is of great persistence in philosophy, to suppose that one of them must be the correct interpretation. Aristotle, like Wisdom, is continually steering us from this temptation when he shows that none of the reductions is satisfactory by itself, but if we take them all together and analyse the

[2] pp. 148–9.
[3] But see his *Philosophy and Psychoanalysis* (Oxford, 1953), pp. 106–7.

relations between them, we can see how the apparent conflict between these accounts can be removed and then how each of them has something to contribute to the true account of the matter. One of the clearest statements in Aristotle's works of this general view of the nature of philosophical method is at *EE* H2, 1245b13–18: 'we must accept the reasoning which will both best explain to us the views held about these matters and will resolve the difficulties and contradictions; and we will achieve this if we show that the conflicting views are held with good reason. For such reasoning will most closely accord with the agreed facts; and it will allow the conflicting views to be retained if analysis can show that each is partly true and partly false'. The words translated 'agreed facts' (*ta phainomena*) are the same as those used in a more familiar passage on method to mark the views of common sense in contrast to the philosophers' paradoxes.[4] There, as has been well argued by Owen,[5] Aristotle's point is to contrast Socrates' view that one cannot act against one's better judgement, with the recognition by common sense that one can so act. In our *EE* passage the force of the expression is the same. Here Aristotle commends the account which recognises and absorbs the conflicting views on the matter under investigation, and which at the same time does not conflict with obvious truths. The emphasis is on the need to eliminate the sense of difficulty which is felt when we are faced with the various conflicting accounts of the matter. This should be done by removing the element of falsity from each account; and we shall then be left with an account which embodies the correct elements in each of the conflicting accounts. For this reason Aristotle says that the conflicting views will be retained; but he will remove the sense of conflict, which arose from the fact that each account has *some* but not *all* of the elements of the true account.

The analysis of the object of wish (*to boulēton*) in *EN* Γ4 provides a clear and illuminating example of the type of metaphysical analysis which is indicated in the programme of *EE* H2. Since I shall discuss this passage in detail, it will be useful to translate it in full:

I have said that wish is for the end. To some it seems to be for the good, to others for what appears good. For those who say that the good is the object of wish, it follows that what is wished by the person who chooses wrongly is not an object of wish (since if it is an object of wish, it will also be good; whereas in the case proposed it was bad). For those, on the

---

[4] *E.N.* H2, 1145b28. Cf. *EE* H1, 1235a31, where this translation is even more clearly preferable to the rendering 'observed facts' (e.g. H. Rackham, *Eudemian Ethics*, London, 1935, p. 365).

[5] 'Tithenai Ta Phainomena' in *Aristote et Les Problèmes de Méthode* (Louvain–Paris, 1961), pp. 85–6.

other hand, who say that what appears good is the object of wish, it follows that there is no natural object of wish but what it seems to each person to be; but different things appear thus to different persons, and it may be that these things are contrary. If these consequences are unsatisfactory, we should say that the good is without qualification and in truth the object of wish, while what appears good is the object of each person's wish – and that the true object of wish is the object of the good man's, while whatever it chances to be is the object of the bad man's. So also in the case of bodies, what is truly healthy is so to those in good condition, while other things are healthy to the ill; and so on with things that are bitter, sweet, hot, heavy, and each of the others. The good man judges each correctly, and in each case what appears to him is truly so. For there are fine and pleasant things special to each condition; and perhaps the most distinctive mark of the good man is that he sees in each case what is true – he is like a standard measure of them. But among the mass of people error seems to come about through pleasure; for it appears to be the good, when it is not. So they choose the pleasant as being the good, and they shun pain as the bad.

In this passage Aristotle notes two plausible answers to the problem of the nature of the object of wish – 'the good' and 'the apparent good'. But although these two answers seem between them to exhaust all the possibilities, each brings paradoxical consequences. For if we say that the good is the object of wish, this brings with it the consequence that the man who wishes something other than the good does not wish at all. That this is paradoxical can be readily seen from the fact that, if we accept the consequence, we are tempted to describe his act of wishing in inverted commas, so that he is said not to *wish* something other than the good but to '*wish*' something other than the good. On the other hand, if we say that the apparent good is the object of wish, this brings with it the consequence that, since different people may have different views of what is the good, there is no such thing as *the* object of wish, but rather there are potentially as many objects of wish as there are people who exercise the faculty. The paradox in this consists in the fact that 'the apparent good' was given as the answer to a question about *the* object of wish; but as an answer it shows that the question was misconceived. For the question was about *the* object of wish, and the effect of the answer is to deny that there is such a thing. The consequences of both the answers – 'the good' and 'the apparent good' – are unacceptable, if we want to be able to say *both* that all cases of wishing really are cases of wishing *and* that not all cases of wishing are directed towards the proper object of wish.

Here, then, we have a dilemma in which both the answers bring intolerable consequences and yet between them seem to exhaust all the possibilities. The situation and Aristotle's remedy for it are of

the sort which are described in *EE* H2. By means of a logical device
he is able to show that, although there is indeed a conflict between
the two unacceptable answers, elements can be extracted from each
to produce an answer which does not generate intolerable consequences. Each answer has some contribution to make to the correct
answer; but because each exaggerates its correct insight to the point
of ignoring the correct insight which the other embodies, neither
is in itself acceptable.

Aristotle distinguishes the unqualified object of wish (*to haplōs
boulēton*) from the object of someone's wish (*to hekastōi boulēton*).
While it is undeniable that each person wishes that which he wishes
(it is because the man who says the good is the object of wish is
forced to deny this, that his account must be rejected), there is no
reason why that which an individual wishes should coincide with
the object of wish. The object of the individual's wish may or may
not coincide with the object of wish; and in fact the two do coincide
in the case of the object of the *good man*'s wish and only in this
case. Thus the good man, or moral expert, is the standard by reference to whose act of wishing we may determine the nature of *the*
object of wish. In the case of all other acts of wishing, observation
only informs us of the nature of the object of *someone*'s wish.

Aristotle illuminates the point by contrasting the man of sound
health with the sick man. The health of the former is enhanced by
what really is healthy and he tastes as sweet what really is sweet;
whereas the latter's health is enhanced by what is healthy *only for
him* and he tastes as sweet what is sweet only to him. What he finds
healthy, or tastes as sweet, is not in fact healthy or sweet. Certainly
what the sick man tastes as sweet is sweet *to the sick man*; but we
can only say that something is sweet without adding such qualifications, if it is tasted as sweet by the man who is the standard in these
matters, the healthy man. We should also note that in the latter case
we say that it is really sweet or a true case of sweetness:[6] to be a case
of real or genuine sweetness is to satisfy the judgement of the expert
in these matters.[7] Further illumination could be gained from a
comparison, which Aristotle does not make in this connection, with
the case of shooting. Shooting and targets are essentially correlative;
without the one the other cannot exist.[8] But only some shots hit the
target; and of those which have failed to hit it we may say that

---

[6] cf. 1113a23, 27.

[7] 1113a29–33.

[8] I exclude from the title of 'shooting' the activity of simply letting the gun
go off with no attempt to aim at a target. The reason why such an activity
is not allowed to be an instance of shooting – or if so, only marginally and
with reservations – is precisely that shooting essentially involves aiming at
targets.

while they *were intended* to be directed at *the* target, they were in fact directed at what they hit, which was therefore *their* target.[9]

Two points should be noted. Firstly, although I have spoken of the expert both in the case of wishing and in the case of tasting sweetness, I do not mean to convey by this that Aristotle necessarily thought it an exclusive or rare accomplishment for a person so to exercise a faculty that the object of *his* faculty should coincide with *the* object of the faculty.[10] Aristotle's use, within a single passage, of the singular to characterise the man whose wish is rightly directed[11] and the plural to characterise those whose taste of sweetness is correct[12] might be thought to indicate that he considers the former form of expertise to be rare and the latter to be common. But nothing turns on this question of numbers. The important distinction is between the successful and the unsuccessful exercise of a faculty. Secondly, it may be thought that the example of the contrast between the man in sound and the man in poor *physical* condition is not fully parallel to the contrast between the man in sound and the man in poor *moral* condition. For in the former case what promotes the health of the sick man *is* good for him and does not merely *seem* good to him; whereas in the latter case the mistaken object of wish is not something which *is* good for him but only something which *seems* good to him. Elsewhere Aristotle shows himself aware of this distinction among the ways in which an attribute can be qualified. At *EN* H12, 1152b29–32, he distinguishes among wrong pleasures those which are 'while bad without qualification, not bad for someone but preferable for him' from those which are 'not even pleasures, but only apparently so'. In the first of these types of qualified pleasures the qualification is made in terms of the *interest* of some individual; some experiences are pleasant for a particular individual but not for people in general. The second type of qualified pleasures must be qualified by reference to the *judgement* of the particular individual who thinks that he finds pleasure in them; of these we can only say that they *seem* pleasant *to someone*, not that the *are* pleasant *tout court*. I am not here concerned with this distinction as it effects the analysis of Pleasure; I introduce it simply to show that Aristotle is aware of the distinction between the two manners of being qualified which seem to be conflated in *EN* Γ4. There is no attempt to distinguish them

---

[9] I have treated this example more fully in my 'Aristotle on Relativism', pp. 199–201. See also G. E. M. Anscombe, 'The Intentionality of Sensation', p. 167.

[10] In what follows I use the word 'faculty' to cover all human functions and activities which we may speak of as directed towards some object outside themselves. Thus the word will cover such diverse activities as knowing, wishing, shooting.

[11] 1113a25, 29.   [12] 1113a26.

in Γ4 because Aristotle's purpose in this chapter is simply to show how the distinction between the qualified and unqualified use of a term can solve the problem about the object of wish.

The distinction qualified/unqualified which we have seen Aristotle use in his analysis of the object of wish is also used by him in the analysis of other central ethical concepts. Thus he appeals to this distinction when he comments on pleasure,[13] the object of friendship,[14] the terrible,[15] the voluntary.[16] He argues that in the case of all these concepts we must recognise a complexity of such a kind that under them fall *both* straightforward instances which stand in need of no further explanation in order to count as instances of the particular concept *and* instances which do need some explicit qualification if they are to count as instances at all. However, of all the places in the two *Ethics* in which this distinction is used, *EN* Γ4 with its analysis of the object of wish is the most illuminating because of the demonstration which it provides of the value of this distinction in unravelling the difficulties left by those whose accounts do not incorporate this distinction. Later I shall argue that the metaphysical theory which is presented in *EN* Γ4 and alluded to in the discussions of certain concepts elsewhere in the *Ethics* is also applied in Aristotle's analysis of certain concepts which are central to his notion of dialectic, and that the character of Aristotle's work on dialectic reflects this metaphysical theory in the same way in which the character of his work on ethics does. Before turning to dialectic, however, it will be useful to consider more fully the general nature of this metaphysical theory.

Something should be said here about my use of the word 'metaphysical'. What is usually understood as falling under the heading 'Aristotle's metaphysics' is the discussion of sensible and non-sensible substance which occurs principally in the *Metaphysics* and the *Physics*. I prefer to classify such discussion under the heading of 'ontology', and to appropriate the name 'metaphysics' for discussions which are concerned with the ultimate grounds of justification for various classes of proposition. I agree with philosophers who argue that discussion of the former kind should be construed as a variant idiom of what is more perspicuously expressed in the latter kind of talk.[17] Be that as it may, the sources for the Aristotelian metaphysical theory which I shall be examining lie not so much in

---

[13] *EN* H12, 1152b27–33; K5, 1176a15–22.
[14] *EN* Θ2, 1155b18–27; Θ5, 1157b25–8.
[15] *EE* Γ1, 1228b18–30.
[16] *EN* Γ1, 1110a18–19.
[17] Cf. John Wisdom, 'The Metamorphosis of Metaphysics' in *Paradox and Discovery* (Oxford, 1965), pp. 57–81, esp. pp. 71–5; Renford Bambrough, 'Principia Metaphysica', *Philosophy* 39 (1964), 101–3.

the *Metaphysics* as in a more scattered series of passages, chief among which is *EN* Γ4. Aristotle has a view of the relation between human faculties and their objects which is of very general application. I believe that the importance and scope of his theory of this matter has been underestimated and neglected, and that it is essential to attend to the varied contexts in which the theory is presented, if we are to have a proper understanding of Aristotle's metaphysics. One effect of this will be a better grasp of the connection between his ideas and those of more recent philosophers whose metaphysical discussion is not carried on in the idiom of ontology.

Aristotle's central insight in the account of wishing is his appreciation that although the faculty and its objects are correlative, each element can independently follow its own logical pattern. Wish is directed towards the good, and each person's wish is directed towards that which he thinks to be the good. These two assertions represent the views of the two opposing parties, and Aristotle accepts them both. But Aristotle indicates his disagreement with both parties when he says that it is possible for the wish of some particular person, viz. the good man, to be directed towards the good, but that the wish of people other than the good man are not directed towards the good. Thus he argues that all cases of wishing really are cases of wishing but that not all are directed towards that which really is the good. One might similarly argue that although all acts of describing are essentially directed towards the producing of descriptions, some acts of describing produce not descriptions but misdescriptions; but nonetheless, acts of describing which produce misdescriptions really are acts of describing. For were this not so, we would be unable to produce an account of the nature of misdescription which showed it to be a *deviation* from the norm of description rather than something positive itself. Similarly, were it not the case that the act of wishing which is directed towards the apparent rather than the real good really is an act of wishing, we would not be justified in calling its object the *apparent* good; for that which is not really an act of wishing must really be something else, and that something else will have its own object, something other than the good, with a real nature of its own. If we suppose in the case of faculties and their objects that where one of the two elements is qualified as real or apparent the other must be qualified in the same way, we lose the value of these qualifications for the analysis of the relation between faculties and their objects. This value lies in the means provided by these qualifications for distinguishing between *successful* or *proper* exercises of a faculty and the *mere* exercise of the faculty.

It is this distinction which is obliterated by each of the two opposing views and preserved in Aristotle's account alone. The view which maintains that the object of wish is the good only allows that successful exercise of a faculty should qualify as exercise; and the view which maintains that the object of wish is the apparent good represents all exercise of the faculty as successful exercise. The obliteration of this distinction is indicative of a distortion on the part of both parties of such a concept as Object-of-Wish. The expression 'object of wish' designates a unitary concept, a fact which is more clearly indicated by the single word Greek expression *boulēton* than in the English translations; and it is a feature of the views which Aristotle attacks that they attempt to drive a wedge between the two elements of such a concept by focusing attention on one of the elements at the expense of the other. Those who make the successful exercise of a faculty the condition of its being an exercise of that faculty at all are so concerned with the objects of the faculty that they forget that the objects are objects *of that faculty*. Those, on the other hand, who regard every exercise of the faculty as equally valid are so concerned with the faculty itself that they forget that correlative to the faculty are objects whose being is logically inseparable from that of the faculty. To revert to the example of shooting and targets, one can say of the former thinkers that they treat the targets as if they could exist without the shooting, and of the latter that they suppose that shooting can exist without targets. The correct account recognises that targets are logically inseparable from shooting and that neither should be considered or explained in isolation from the other.

Ambiguity

It is tempting, but incorrect, to diagnose such expressions as 'object of wish' as simply ambiguous between the two (supposed) senses 'what *ought to be* wished' and 'what *is* wished'.[18] If this ambiguity really were present, Aristotle's argument against his opponents would fail; for the one – he who maintains that the object of wish is the good – could claim that he is talking about what *ought to be* wished, while the other – he who maintains that the object of wish is the apparent good – could claim that he is talking about what *is* wished. In the face of these claims Aristotle's analysis of the situation as one in which a fundamental conflict between two answers to the same question can only be resolved by adopting a *via media* which offers an answer distinct from either, would be ill-founded. In fact Aristotle's analysis has precisely the effect of expelling the temptation to see such an ambiguity here. It is, of course, true that there

18 Alternatively, in terms of 'wishing *for*' the two senses would become 'what is wished for' and 'what is wished': this is how W. F. R. Hardie, *Aristotle's Ethical Theory*, pp. 168–9, diagnoses the ambiguity.

may be a difference between that which any particular person actually wishes and that which ought to be wished, and Aristotle recognises this difference with his distinction between the unqualified and qualified object of wish. But he argues that what ought to be wished by any person at all is the same; it is something objective and common to all wishing subjects. That this is so is shown by our readiness to say that what everybody *really* wishes is the same (although individuals may mistakenly think that their wishes are private and personal). *The* object of wish, then, is what ought to be wished, and as such it is not open to any qualification which may arise from the variety to be found among the subjects who exercise the faculty of wish. But when we consider what is actually wished by the various individuals who exercise the faculty, qualification is necessary in those cases where they actually wish something other than that which ought to be wished. These are precisely the cases in which Aristotle finds the notion of the qualified object of wish indispensable; for it is in these cases that we must say that what they actually wish is not *the* object of wish but the object of *their* wish. So Aristotle's account recognises and absorbs the distinction between what ought to be wished and what is wished. Moreover it shows that the metaphysical importance of the distinction lies solely in its being able to make clear that where the distinction is relevant, this can be achieved by adding to the expression 'object of wish' a qualification which is not needed where it is not relevant. But the central case of wishing an object is that done by the good man, whose wishing is such as to measure up to the value of the object of the faculty. He wishes as he ought to and what ought to be wished: others do not wish as they ought to, and for this reason the objects of *their* wishes are other than what ought to be wished.

To get a better understanding of this important point, it will be useful to consider the concept of Taste. The analysis of this concept illustrates Aristotle's metaphysical theory in a way which is perhaps more accessible to the English reader than is the case with the examples, such as the object of wish, with which Aristotle works. As in the case of the object of wish, so also with taste one finds a dispute between the extreme realist, who regards taste as something not necessarily possessed by everyone but confined to those who show excellence and expertise, and the extreme relativist, who regards taste as something possessed, and possessed in equal degree, by everyone. The realist denies that the man whose taste is bad has taste at all, and is driven to the extreme of regarding the expression 'bad taste' as a contradiction; the relativist asserts that the man whose taste is bad does have taste, and is driven to the extreme of not recognising any grounds for valuing taste as good or bad. Here again it is tempting to diagnose as the cause of the dispute an ambiguity in the word 'taste', of such a kind that in one use, that on which the realist exclusively concentrates, it means 'good judgement', while in another use, that on which the relativist exclusively concentrates, it means simply 'the exercise of judgement'.[19] This appeal to the ambiguity of 'taste' may easily allow the dispute to dissolve under the excuse of exaggeration and neglect on the part of both parties. According to this account, the contradiction between 'bad taste is not taste' – the assertion of the realist – and 'taste may be bad' – the assertion of the relativist – is only apparent; for if we recognise the ambiguity of 'taste', we can see that it is not the case that the realist denies and the relativist asserts the same attribute of the same subject, viz. 'taste' of 'bad taste'. Similarly, one may allow a dispute as to whether grass grows on banks to dissolve as only an apparent disagreement, when it is realised that the disputant who challenged the assertion was in fact meaning by 'bank' the place where money is changed.

But this account, in turn, is misleading. We may accept that the contradiction between the two assertions 'bad taste is not taste' and 'taste may be bad' is indeed only apparent, since both assertions are in fact true. But it would be a mistake to deduce from this that the accounts of taste of which each of these assertions is an expression are acceptable. That neither is acceptable is readily seen from the fact that each denies a true assertion which the other makes. By contrast, we would be able to accept an account which followed the lines of Aristotle's account of the object of wish, since this would not be open to the objection that it denies something which is true. Such an account would accommodate both the assertions about taste by making *taste* (unqualified) something that may, but need not, coincide with qualified taste, i.e. with taste qualified as *someone*'s taste or *bad* taste. Accordingly, there are cases of taste where it is not necessary to add any qualification, cases which come up to the common standard of excellence; this was denied by the relativist when he argued that all cases are necessarily qualified by reference to their owner and that no case has a greater claim to the title of 'taste' than any other. But also we must allow that there are cases of bad taste and that the expression 'bad taste' is not self-contradictory; this was denied by the realist when he argued that only

---

[19] It would be possible for those who urge this account to appeal to the distinction in the *Oxford English Dictionary* between senses iii 7 and iii 8 of 'Taste'. He could point to iii 7 – 'the fact or condition of liking or preferring something; inclination, liking for' – as the sense which the relativist intends by 'taste', and to iii 8 – 'the sense of what is appropriate, harmonious, or beautiful; *esp.* the discernment and appreciation of the beautiful in nature or art; *spec.* the faculty of perceiving and enjoying what is excellent in art, literature and the like' – as the sense which the realist intends by 'taste'.

cases of good taste can qualify as cases of taste at all. Insofar as characterisation of the word 'taste' as simply ambiguous suggests that it is possible to isolate two distinct senses which the word can bear in its various occurrences, the analysis of taste which follows the pattern of Aristotle's analysis of the object of wish tells against the characterisation. For in the case of typically ambiguous words, such as 'bank', the distinct types of object which the word covers in its various senses all have a fully justified claim to be designated by that word. But in the case of 'taste', 'object of wish' and other words or expressions which I shall examine later in this chapter, we must distinguish between objects which have a fully justified claim to be designated by the word and objects which have a tenuous claim, a claim which can only be justified if we add the necessary qualification when we use the word to describe them. This is what is brought out by the Aristotelian analysis and missed by the types of analysis with which it is contrasted. This analysis suggests that instead of describing the words as ambiguous, we would be less likely to mislead if we were to describe them as used with varying degrees of justification to cover not only the central cases but also peripheral cases which can only be justified as cases at all by referring to the central cases.[20]

Universality

In chapter two I commented briefly on the relation between central and peripheral cases when I discussed the types of universality which Aristotle claims for ontology and dialectic respectively.[21] I argued that ontology should be regarded as universal in the way in which Wealth is, while dialectic should be regarded as universal in the way in which Being Someone's Wealth is. Aristotle finds it necessary when characterising ontology as universal to qualify this universality by adding 'in the sense that it is primary'; and I maintained that this qualification is necessary because Aristotle realises that he is using the notion of universality in a way which is opposed to its normal use – a use whereby a character is universal if it can be shown to apply *fully and equally* to a number of distinct instances. That which is universal as primary cannot so apply to all the instances which it covers, since it applies to some instances fully but

---

[20] This suggestion recalls the analysis of such words as 'being' and 'medical' which Aristotle gives at *Met.* Γ2, 1003a33–1003b10, and which formed an important element in G. E. L. Owen's thesis (examined on pp. 42–9 above) that Aristotle's concept of a universal dialectic antedates the general science proposed in the *Metaphysics*. For doubt as to whether such an analysis reveals ambiguity in these words, see J. Hintikka, *Time and Necessity* (Oxford, 1973), pp. 21–5.

[21] pp. 44–5 above.

to others only in an extended and qualified way. I shall argue that in extending the notion of universality in this way Aristotle does not distort the notion as it is found in its more familiar form; rather he develops features of the notion which it always possessed and which justify his extension of it when he seeks to apply it in the case of certain complex concepts.

This extended notion, and the contrast between it and the more simple notion from which it is developed, gain illumination when considered in connection with the concepts which I have been discussing – taste, object of wish etc. Within the concept of taste it might seem that what is universal is being *someone*'s taste, i.e. the form of taste which is possessed by all subjects who have their own taste, be it good or bad. It is, after all, true of all cases of taste, including the cases of bad taste, that they are *cases* of taste; and for this reason we are inclined to see as the universal element in taste what is common to all cases of taste, the fact that they are *someone*'s taste. But equally, and contrarily, one can argue that what is common to all cases of taste is that they are cases of *taste*, not cases of *someone*'s taste. For the qualification introduced by saying that the taste is that of some particular individual has the effect of *distinguishing* the various instances of taste; its effect is to diversify rather than to unify these instances. But the universal is essentially that element in the collection of the instances which unifies them, and this consideration points to the location of the universal element not in being someone's taste but in taste. However, we have already seen that taste, as opposed to his own taste, is not something which is necessarily possessed by each individual who has his own taste. It is, rather, something the possession of which is restricted to the expert;[22] consequently it does not cover all the cases for which we are seeking the unifying element and which *are* covered by the concept of being someone's taste.[23] For this reason, as I noted above, Taste fails to fulfil one of the requirements for being the universal element. On the other hand, the notion of the universal as the one over the many is itself derived from the more basic notion of the universal as that element in things which must be apprehended if we are to understand and explain the particular instances which it covers. This second notion of the universal is the dominant one in Plato's theory of Forms; for the Forms are primarily objects of knowledge and only secondarily universals in the sense of being common characteristics. This is clear particularly from the hesitation

---

[22] For the implications of the use of the word 'expert' here, see p. 58 above.

[23] The complexity here is closely related to that noted by J. L. Austin in arguments for the existence of universals; see 'Are There *A Priori* Concepts?', *Philosophical Papers* (Oxford, 1961), pp. 2–5.

which is felt at *Parm.* 130c about allowing that there are Forms of such things as a Man or Fire; for these would be used as stock examples by the modern philosopher who appealed to the distinction between common characteristics and the individuals which share them, in order to expound the theory of universals.

Aristotle too, for all his disagreement with Plato on the ontology of universals, regards the universal as that on which the mind must focus if we are to understand things.[24] According to this notion of the universal it is the object of the expert's attention and something the apprehension of which underpins the expert's claim for the objective truth of his own comments as against the subjectivity which attends the comments of those who do not have access to these objects. This line of argument clearly points to taste, rather than being someone's taste, as the universal. For it is the expert's taste which alone can be called *taste*, and only experts can be relied upon to agree in matters of taste; for insofar as those for whom expertise is claimed disagree, precisely is the claim for their expertise made subject to doubt. The idea that the taste of experts is essentially *one* provides essential support for the claim that objectivity is possible in matters of taste; and the demand that objective judgement should be possible provides the basic impetus in the search for universals. So to designate *taste* as the universal element in all the cases of being someone's taste, despite the fact that not all these are cases of *taste*, is no abuse of the notion of the universal. Taste is the only genuinely unifying element in the whole collection of instances of taste. This is shown by the fact that if we wish to argue that there can be objectivity in matters of taste, i.e. that rational progress towards unanimity of judgement is in principle possible, we must appeal to the nation of *expert* taste, which is the only form of taste which has an unqualified claim to the name.

The same analysis holds when we consider the universal element in the case of the object of wish. What is public and common to a number of different acts of wishing is that they are directed to the same object. If the object of my wish differs from the object of wish, this means that my act of wishing is something private and individual and that its object is not universal. When it is necessary, in speaking of the object of an exercise of the faculty, to introduce a qualification and speak of it as the object of *someone*'s wish, this indicates a specification and individuation of the object; but in those cases where the qualification is not necessary, i.e. where the faculty is directed towards *the* object of wish, we have an object which is common to all wishing subjects and one which, even though it may not be actually be wished by them, is potentially open to all of them.

[24] *Met.* Z15, 1039b27–1040a7; *An. Post.* A24, 86a3–10.

As I noted above,[25] we are inclined to say of anyone who exercises the faculty of wish that what he *really* wishes is the good, i.e. *the* object of wish which is the same for all subjects. So it is *the* object of wish which is common to a number of distinct instances and which makes it possible for objectivity to be attained in the exercise of the faculty of wish; and for these reasons it does not put excessive strain on language to call it universal.

It can be argued to be primary in all the senses of 'primary' which Aristotle recognises. The notion of the object of wish is a necessary part of the notion of being the object of someone's wish, since the latter is distinguished from the former by its *appearing* to be what the former *really is*. This corresponds to Aristotle's notion of logical priority.[26] Similarly, we can only say what really is the object of anyone's wish if we know what *the* object of wish is; and this corresponds to Aristotle's notions of epistemological and ontological priority.[27] It should cause no surprise that these criteria for priority are satisfied by the object of wish. For Aristotle's argument in *Met.* Z1 is designed to support the claim that substance is reality, and the argument derives its main weight from the fact that substance is prior to other types of existing things in the various ways given above. Evidently, then, these forms of priority are marks of reality; and since the object of wish is contrasted with the object of someone's wish as reality is contrasted with appearance, it is natural that *the* object of wish should be prior in these ways to the individual objects of wish. I conclude, then, that the expression which Aristotle uses to describe the place of theology among the sciences – 'universal in the sense that it is primary' – can apply equally to the sort of universality which the object of wish possesses among the various objects of various persons' wishes.

I have tried to bring out the philosophical value of Aristotle's analysis of the 'object of wish'. It is an analysis which avoids the pitfalls both of extreme realism and of extreme relativism by keeping in proper perspective the parts played both by the faculties themselves and by their objects in the exercise of the faculties. It shares with realism the property of maintaining that correlative to the faculty there is an object which is logically independent of any particular exercise of the faculty, and so of upholding the existence of *objective* grounds for according different value to different instances of the exercise of the faculty. It shares with relativism the recognition that the faculty itself is essentially connected with its objects and that accordingly attention must be focussed on the

[25] p. 62.
[26] See *Met.* Z1, 1028a34–6; M2, 1077b4–11, – *x* is logically prior to *y* if the definition of *y* must contain the definition of *x*.
[27] *Met.* Z1, 1028a31–4, 1028a36–1028b2.

quality of the subject who exercises the faculty if we are to place a valuation on the judgement which issues from the exercise of the faculty. But Aristotle's analysis corrects the two extreme accounts by giving due recognition to elements in the situation which each had ignored. It thereby both resolves the difficulty which had produced the two conflicting accounts, and avoids the paradoxes to which each of these accounts had given rise.

On being more intelligible

Aristotle's analysis of the object of wish is capable of very wide application; and I want now to examine how he extends it to certain concepts which play a prominent part in his account of dialectic. I have already argued that the way to understand the notion of dialectic itself and its relation to other forms of intellectual activity lies in applying this sort of analysis to the whole concept of intellectual activity. I wish now to reinforce the earlier argument by showing that certain specific concepts which Aristotle uses in his exposition of the nature and practice of dialectic in the *Topics* and *SE* also conform to this pattern of analysis and are clearly shown by Aristotle to do so.

When he comments on method in science Aristotle frequently draws a distinction between what is more intelligible *absolutely* and what is more intelligible *to us*.[28] We have already seen that this contrast appears in the *De Philosophia*,[29] and in the treatises it appears in a wide variety of contexts.[30] Aristotle appears to be in some doubt as to what is to be regarded as more intelligible in either of these two ways, since he says in some places that the more general and universal is more intelligible absolutely and the less general is more intelligible to us,[31] but in others that the particular is more intelligible absolutely and the more general is more intelligible to us.[32] However, he consistently maintains that the proper course in

---

28 *Ta gnōrimōteron haplōs* and *ta gnōrimōteron hēmin*. The justification for this translation of 'gnōrimon' will appear in the analysis which follows. Aristotle also speaks of men as 'gnōrimoi'; and in political contexts this may best be translated 'notable'. But I maintain that in dialectical contexts (e.g. *Top.* A1, 100b23; A10, 104a10) a *gnōrimos* is so called paronymously from the *gnōrima* which he understands; so here the word should be translated 'man of understanding'. Similar considerations of paronymy govern the translation of 'endoxon' and 'endoxos' (see pp. 77–85 below).
29 Fr. 8 (Ross, *Fragmenta*); *cf.* p. 8 above.
30 See Bonitz, *Index* 159a33–8. Bonitz does not record the important occurrence of the distinction at *Top.* Z4, 141a26–142a21, which is discussed below.
31 *An. Post.* A2, 71b33–72a5.
32 *Phys.* A1, 184a16–184b14, esp. 184a23–4, 'so one should progress from universal to particular things'.

conducting an investigation is to start from what is more intelligible
to us, but less intelligible absolutely, and proceed to what is more
intelligible absolutely, but (before we start the investigation) less
intelligible to us.[33] This distinction between forms of greater intelligibility has received little emphasis from commentators on Aristotle's theory of scientific method, and this is probably due to the
fact that in most of the passages where the distinction is used
Aristotle gives no indication of the philosophical problems and
disputes which may have lain behind it. However, since we find in
the *Ethics* a discussion – that of the object of wish in *EN* Γ4 –
which shows the value of this distinction in resolving problems about
one ethical concept and which, therefore, helps us to appreciate its
force when Aristotle uses it in connection with other, less fully
explored, ethical concepts, we may expect that in some context
Aristotle will provide a similarly illuminating demonstration of its
value in connection with intellectual concepts. This expectation is
increased when we notice that in a number of passages Aristotle
indicates a connection between the logic of Good and that of
Intelligible.[34]

In fact the expectation is fulfilled by the discussion of intelligibility
at *Top.* Z4, 141a26–142a16. The topic of intelligibility is the first to
be discussed among those which consider whether a proposed
definition is the definition at all, as opposed to whether the definition has been presented well;[35] and together with the topic of
priority, with which it is closely connected,[36] it occupies the whole
of Z4. The discussion opens with the argument that the definition
must contain elements which are more intelligible than the
definiendum. For such a definition is clearly better than one which
does not contain more intelligible elements, since the purpose of
definition is to instruct; and because the essence of each subject is
single, so must its definition be single. Consequently there is no
room for variations in degree among definitions, and we can allow
only the *best* definition to be *the* definition.[37] But at this point
Aristotle introduces the distinction between that which is more
intelligible absolutely and that which is more intelligible to us. He
notes that although the prior is more intelligible absolutely than the
posterior, *we* may find the posterior more intelligible, for the reason
that the posterior is more accessible to sense experience.[38] Accordingly, the earlier argument about the intelligibility of the elements
of the definition must be refined to accommodate this distinction,

---

[33] *De An.* B2, 413a11; *Met.* Z3, 1029b3–12.
[34] *Met.* Z3, 1029b5–8. At *EN* A4, 1095b2–8, the distinction between the two
forms of intelligibility is applied to a problem of method in ethics.
[35] 141a23–5. [36] 141a26, 141b6, 142a17.
[37] 141a26–141b2. [38] 141b3–14.

and this Aristotle does in 141b15–142a16. He allows that although the definition which contains elements which are prior is better absolutely than one which does not, one should present to opponents who do not find the prior more intelligible a definition which contains elements which are more intelligible *to them*.[39] This follows from the premiss that the purpose of definition is to instruct, a premiss which in the opening argument was used to support the claim that the elements of the definition must be more intelligible than the definiendum. However, Aristotle reasserts the conclusion of the opening argument, that there can be only one real definition of each subject,[40] and he provides some arguments for this which use the distinction between the two forms of intelligibility.[41] Nevertheless, he concludes his analysis by noting that just as in matters of the body there is a difference between the absolutely healthy, which gives health to those who are sound physically, and the relatively healthy, which gives health only to those who deviate from the norm of physical fitness, so also in matters of the mind there is a difference between that which is intelligible to those who are sound mentally – the absolutely intelligible – and that which is intelligible to those who deviate from the norm of mental fitness. We must take account of this difference when we present definitions and must consider it in relation to our opponents, just as (although Aristotle does not explicitly make this point) in matters of medicine we must take into account the physical state of the patient when we advise him on what will promote his health.[42]

In all this discussion there is no reference to the views of others. But the remarks which close the section indicate that the distinction between the two forms of intelligibility, although in all probability an Aristotelian discovery since there is no evidence for any other provenance, reflects a distinction which must to some extent have made itself felt in current debate on the problems of definition. Aristotle says that 'we must make precise each of these distinctions and use them in our dialectic to the best advantage; and *agreement* that the definition has been refuted will be most readily secured if the account' (*scil.* that of one's opponent) 'contains elements that are more intelligible neither absolutely nor to us'.[43] The mention here of the ease with which agreement can be secured to the refutation of definitions which contain elements which are prior in *neither* of the two ways strongly suggests that Aristotle found in current dialectic a situation in which some people required that the elements of the definition be more intelligible in one of the two ways, while others required that they be more intelligible in the other way. Here we should remember the comment of *EN* A4, 1095a32–1095b1, that

[39] 141b15–22. [40] 141b22–142a9. [41] 141b34–142a6.
[42] 142a9–13. [43] 142a12–16.

Plato debated whether investigation should proceed *to* or *from* the first principles; this comment is immediately followed by the distinction between the two forms of intelligibility, and it suggests that Plato was aware of the sort of problem which Aristotle uses the distinction to resolve. However, although Aristotle does not in *Top.* Z4 appeal explicitly to the difficulties resulting from the theories of others which the distinction can resolve, the construction of the argument of the chapter allows us to extract easily a dilemma of the same form as that which provides the starting-point for the analysis of the object of wish in *EN* Γ4.

Once again we can construct two analyses of the role of intelligibility in definition; and these analyses will lead their proponents into the paradoxical extremes of either realism or relativism. One party to the debate maintains that the subject of definition is the essence and that this is single, and so does not allow that anything can be a definition if it does not provide the essence. The other party maintains that the purpose of definition is to instruct us about the nature of the subject, and so he allows as a definition anything which in fact does so instruct us. The former position moves to extreme realism when it is forced to deny the title of definition to an account which does in fact instruct us about the nature of the subject; and yet the assertion that the definition must provide the essence had been supported by the argument that the elements of the essence are more intelligible than the subject and thus such as to be instructive about its nature.[44] In this way the extreme realist overreaches himself. So also does the extreme relativist who embraces the consequences of the alternative account of definitions. For he is forced to discount the grounds for distinguishing in merit one instructive account of the subject's nature from any other. Since such grounds derive from the fidelity with which the subject is portrayed, relativism is forced to admit accounts without concern for the subject's nature and, in its most extreme form, to deny that the subject has one. Here too, then, the focus of excessive attention on one part of the notion of being instructive about the subject's nature has eliminated consideration of the other part of that notion.

So we have a situation similar to that in which the two conflicting accounts of the object of wish were found to be unsatisfactory. In both cases the positions of the realist and the relativist are extreme because they obliterate the distinction between the performance of an exercise and the successful or skilful performance of that exercise; for the realist only successful performance counts as performance at all, and the relativist excludes the possibility of any performance being more successful than any other.

In resolving the problem of definitions the distinction between

[44] 141b25–34.

the absolute and the relative, i.e. between the unqualified and the qualified uses of the expression 'more intelligible', is employed. Aristotle's account preserves the requirement, on which both the conflicting accounts were based, that the definition should be instructive. On the other hand, Aristotle argues that although it is indeed the case that *the* definition must contain elements which are absolutely more intelligible than the definiendum, we may say that the expression which contains elements which *someone finds* more intelligible is a definition *for him*.[45] By his distinction between the unqualified and the qualified uses of the expression 'more intelligible' Aristotle is able to introduce a similar distinction into the uses of the words 'definition' and 'instructive', so that the true insights which are present in the accounts of both the realist and the relativist are not lost. For the former appreciated the absolute and unconditional nature of *the* definition; and this is reflected in Aristotle's argument that *the* definition must contain elements which are unconditionally more intelligible than the definiendum. The latter appreciated that the notions of instruction and intelligibility necessarily involve the notion of a person who will be instructed and will understand; and this is reflected in Aristotle's argument that not only is that which is intelligible in a qualified way intelligible to someone – the man of unsound mental disposition – but also that which is intelligible in an unqualified way is intelligible *to someone* – the man of *sound* mental disposition.[46]

This last point is of great importance, since it shows how Aristotle's analysis differs from the other two. Aristotle argues that despite the diversity which can infect the object of the faculty – in this case, the object of understanding – when reference is made to the subject who exercises it, there is nevertheless one case of the exercise of the faculty when reference to the subject is possible but not necessary. This is the case where the subject who exercises the faculty of understanding is the man of sound mental disposition. In ethical matters the moral expert is the man who recognises a given property in what really has the property, and in medical matters the man of sound physical disposition finds healthy what really is so;[47] and likewise where understanding is concerned, it is the man of sound mental disposition who finds more intelligible that which really is so. Because what he finds more intelligible really is so, it is not necessary to qualify the objects of his understanding as objects

[45] cf. 141b19, 23.

[46] 142a9–11.

[47] For a clear statement of the relation between appearance and reality in ethical matters, cf. *EN* K5, 1176a15–16, 'evidently in all such cases what appears to the good man *is*'. This expresses forcefully Aristotle's belief that reality (*einai*) and appearance (*phainesthai*) do not exclude each other.

of *his* understanding, although such qualification *is* necessary when we comment on the objects of anyone else's understanding. This is the point which Aristotle makes against the relativist. But although it is not *necessary* to qualify the objects of the mentally sound man's understanding, it is *possible* so to qualify them. This is the point which he makes against the realist. For the realist who lacks the distinction between the two forms of intelligibility supposes that any claim for intelligibility other than for absolute intelligibility cannot be allowed; and so he excludes the possibility of mentioning the subject for whom the absolutely more intelligible is more intelligible, lest the absoluteness of its greater intelligibility be infringed by referring the intelligibility to a *particular* person or group of people. If we are to understand Aristotle's analysis of the matter, it is crucial to appreciate that, for all the realism which undoubtedly characterises his account,[48] he disagrees with the extreme realist in maintaining that the absolutely intelligible is intelligible to a particular group of people, and that *the* definition is one which will be instructive to this group. It is because Aristotle does not regard the categories of absolute and relative as incompatible that the *purely* relative definition, which contains elements which *must* be qualified as more intelligible *to someone* and which must itself be qualified as a definition *ad hominem*, is still allowed to be a definition.

So we may sum up the argument of *Top.* Z4 by saying that *the* definition – the proper or real definition – is that which proceeds in terms of the absolutely more intelligible and provides us with the unqualified object of understanding; but an account which proceeds in terms of what is more intelligible only to some particular person or group of people and provides them with objects only of *their* understanding, is not to be denied the title of definition, albeit definition qualified by reference to those whom it instructs.

Other logico-dialectical concepts

I should argue that the argument of *Top.* Z4 is invaluable for the understanding not only of the distinction between the two forms of intelligibility but also of a whole range of concepts which Aristotle uses in his theory of scientific method. Of all the passages where Aristotle uses the distinction between the two forms of intelligibility, it is *Top.* Z4 which shows most clearly the problems which he uses the distinction to resolve; and this chapter also helps us to understand the purpose of the distinction when it is applied to other concepts related to that of intelligibility. At *Met.* K5, 1062a2–11,

---

[48] *The* definition is that which expresses the real nature of the definiendum, 141b22–5.

73

30–1, Aristotle distinguishes absolute demonstration from demonstration *ad hominem*,[49] and uses the distinction to show that it is possible to demonstrate something which the rules of *demonstration* show to be indemonstrable. Similarly at *SE* 8, 170a12–19, a distinction is drawn between syllogisms and refutations which have to be qualified by reference to the man against whom they are directed and those which do not need this qualification.

Quite generally the distinction is fundamental to the philosophy of logic. For such concepts as proof, argument, inference, all contain a reference to the *subjects* who exercise or experience these things. The study of logic seeks to free these concepts from their dependence on the subjects and to establish theses about them which are *objectively* and universally valid; and only if it can achieve this do we allow that the study of logic is a skilful activity. However, despite this claim for objectivity which logic must make if it is to be counted as a skill, it must not be forgotten that the concepts with which it deals cannot lose the reference which they essentially contain to subjects. It is impossible for something to be a proof if it is such that it could be conceived not to be convincing *to anyone*. This does not mean that to be counted as proof it must convince some actually existing person, only that there must be some *conceivable* person who would be convinced; and this conceivable person is, once again, the expert in matters of logic. Aristotle was well aware of this. He applies to the logical concepts of demonstration and syllogism the distinction between absolute and relative which, as we have seen, underlies a general metaphysical theory which expresses this awareness. Moreover an important part is played in the theory of syllogism by the notion of *being obvious*. The validity of the imperfect syllogisms – those in the second and third figures – is demonstrated by reducing them to the syllogisms of the first figure, the perfection of which consists precisely in the fact that *we can readily see* the necessity which characterises their inferences.[50]

Nevertheless, when he presents his theory of inference in the *Prior Analytics* Aristotle is mainly concerned to stress the absolute validity of the theses which he argues; and this is what we should expect in a work which seeks to present a logical theory of objective and universal validity. If we wish to find due weight given to the subjective element in the logical concepts, we must turn to Aristotle's comments on dialectic and rhetoric; for these are activities

---

[49] '*Apodeixis haplōs*' and '*pros tonde*'; cf. *Met.* Δ5, 1015b6–9, 'if he has demonstrated *haplōs*'.

[50] cf. *An. Pr.* A1, 24b22–4, 'I call a syllogism perfect if it requires nothing other than the premisses in order for the necessity to be obvious'. G. Patzig makes this point well in his analysis of the distinction between perfect and imperfect inferences, in *Die Aristotelische Syllogistik*, pp. 56–8.

which essentially involve other *actual* people, while the concepts of pure logic contain a reference only to an *ideal* cognitive subject. This theoretical distinction between the forms of subjectivity which characterise the use of logical concepts in dialectic and in pure logic should not obscure the fact that *in practice* the observation of the reactions of actual people is an indispensable aid to the calculation of the reactions of an ideal person. I propose now to examine some of the passages which indicate Aristotle's recognition of the importance of the part played by the subjective category in some of the central concepts of dialectic.

It is natural that Aristotle should emphasise the importance of the cognitive subject when he discusses the concepts of dialectic; for, as he says at *Top.* Θ1, 155b10, 'all this sort of thing is relative to another person'. The dialectical exercise necessarily involves two people; and from this it follows that in recommending that the dialectician employ certain concepts Aristotle must draw attention to the subjective element in these concepts. In dialectic, success is achieved when one has secured the agreement of a particular opponent.[51] To secure this agreement one must produce a sense of conviction, but one must produce it in a particular person; and while it may be true that a sense of conviction is most likely to be produced by that which is really convincing, there is no guarantee that any individual will be convinced by this. Pure logic is not concerned with the vagaries of the individual's reaction, and indeed in its search for objectivity it is positively prohibited from considering the individual as such. But dialectic is necessarily concerned with the individual and his logical reactions, since in the practice of dialectic it is only with individuals that one can deal.

Nevertheless, Aristotle recognises that it is impossible to consider the varying reactions of all individuals. As he says at *SE* 9, 170b5–8, the list which he has given of the sources of apparent refutations will give us a grasp of those which 'appear not to anyone but to such-and-such persons (*tois toioisde*); for all the factors which make them apparent to chance persons are indeterminate for an investigator'. In this context Aristotle is arguing that the concept of dialectic imposes limit and order on what would otherwise be a formless

---

[51] This view of the nature of dialectic is implicit in almost every page of the *Topics*, to such an extent that Aristotle does not feel the need to make explicit comment on it. But for a particularly clear indication that securing the agreement of a particular opponent is essential to the dialectical exercise, cf. the homonymy topics: *Top.* B3, 110a23–110b15, where the need for agreement is indicated at 110a33, 37, 110b3, and the reference to a particular opponent is given at 110a27; and *Top.* Z10, 148a23–148b22, where the need to note the linguistic distinctions which one's opponent makes, and to exploit his failures to make these distinctions, is repeatedly emphasised.

mass of sophistic material.[52] Therefore Waitz supposes that the contrast between persons mentioned in this passage is one between dialecticians and the rest.[53] But this interpretation, which is anyway implausible since dialecticians, as such, would seem the group least likely to be taken in by apparent argument, is excluded by comparison with a parallel comment in the *Rhetoric*. Here Aristotle is examining the central concept of rhetoric, the persuasive;[54] and after noting that what is persuasive is essentially persuasive *to someone*, he continues:

No art considers the individual. For example medicine considers what is healthy not for Socrates or Callias but for such-and-such a person or persons (*tois toioisde*), since this is a matter of art whereas the individual is indefinite and unknowable. Nor will rhetoric consider what is plausible (*endoxon*) to an individual, such as Socrates or Hippias, but what is so to *such-and-such* people, as does dialectic. For this too does not reason from chance views (*Rhet*. A2, 1356b30–6).

This passage throws valuable light on dialectic in a number of ways which will be discussed later. For our present purpose it establishes, against Waitz' interpretation, that the meaning of '*tois toioisde*' in both passages is 'such-and-such persons'; and this gives us important information on the aims of dialecticians. For it is clear that in *Rhet*. A2 Aristotle is contrasting the art which pays attention to the views of each individual, however eccentric these views be, with that which organises and selects certain views as typical and specially relevant to the subject under consideration. The marked similarities of language between what he says in this chapter and in *SE* 9, coupled with the fact that there is an explicit reference to dialectic, show that in both chapters the theory of art is the same.

Both *SE* 9 and *Rhet*. A2 show a full recognition of the fact that the concepts of the persuasive and the apparent syllogism, which form respectively part of the province of rhetoric and dialectic, are essentially relative concepts. The persuasive must persuade *someone*, and the apparent syllogism must appear to someone to be a syllogism. We have already seen that this element of relativity and subjectivity characterises all the concepts in ethics and dialectic which have been discussed in this chapter, and that it is not incompatible with the claim that these concepts can assume an absolute form, in which case they are designated by an unqualified use of the corresponding expression: the object of wish is the object of some-

---

[52] *SE* 170a34–9, 170b8–11, 172b5–8. I have commented on this idea on pp. 39–40 above.

[53] *Aristotelis Organon*, vol. 2, p. 546.

[54] *To pithanon*. For this as the central concept of rhetoric, see *Rhet*. A1, 1355b8–17; A2, 1355b25–34, 'so let rhetoric be a faculty for considering in each case what can be persuasive'.

one's wish. In the case of these two concepts, however, Aristotle contrasts his position with that of the extreme relativist by maintaining not that the concept should be studied in its absolute and unqualified form, but that it should be studied in its qualified form; qualified by reference not to random individuals but to types of individual which are selected as specially relevant. The study of apparent syllogisms must be organised on the basis of some selection among the varieties of ways in which people may be deceived; and it is this organisation and selection which makes this study an *art*. A science must study a concept in its absolute form in order to achieve the objectivity and universality which must characterise a science. For only in this form does it relate to an object which is not dependent on the varying perspectives of the individuals who view it; and science must remove these distortions of perspective. On the other hand, the arts – dialectic, rhetoric, medicine – *are* concerned with the individual perspectives as well as with that which is seen through, and distorted by, them. But the arts too seek to achieve universality and objectivity; and they can do this, in a way which is different from that of the sciences and which reflects their nature as arts, by abstracting from the total of individual perspectives those which are of special interest for some reason. The reasons will vary, but we may broadly distinguish two types: the views or reactions may be interesting because they are those of the majority, or they may be interesting because they come from some specially well-qualified individual or group.[55] However, the important point at present is that Aristotle regards it as characteristic of an art that it should indeed consider the reactions of different people, in which it is contrasted with the sciences, but it should not consider them indiscriminately and without abstracting from the all the available reactions, in which it is contrasted with the absence of art.

Endoxa

The notion of the apparent syllogism is rather marginal to the main area of dialectic; for its place is in sophistic, which is an offshoot of dialectic.[56] But a notion which is central to dialectic is that of the *endoxon*. Aristotle defines the dialectical syllogism as one which takes its start from *endoxa*, in contrast to the demonstrative syllogism which takes its start from what is primary and true.[57] The translation of *endoxon* presents difficulties. Pickard-Cambridge[58] renders it 'opinions that are generally accepted', whereas Tricot[59] renders it

[55] *Top.* A1, 100b21–3, discussed p. 79 below.
[56] *SE* 2, 165b7–8; 11, 171b34–7; *Rhet.* A1, 1355b15–21.
[57] *Top.* A1, 100a27–30; *SE* 2, 165b1–4.
[58] Oxford Translation.   [59] *Topiques*.

'prémisses probables'. The most useful discussion is that of Le Blond[60] who recognises that the word bears both of these senses, and argues that they can be combined into a single coherent notion. Le Blond, however, makes no mention of the distinction, which is drawn at *Top.* Θ5, 159b1, between the unqualified and qualified *endoxon*, and I shall argue that this distinction is of great importance in understanding the notion.

Le Blond first isolates the sense of 'probabilitié intrinsèque, objective'. But it is doubtful whether the notion of objective probability should be regarded as one of the main components of the sense of the word. The only passage in Aristotle which seems to point to this sense is *An. Pr.* B27, where a probability (*eikos*) is defined as 'an endoxic premiss' and said to be what people know to happen (or not to happen) for the most part,[61] and a sign is defined as 'a demonstrative premiss which is either necessary or endoxic'.[62] Aristotle devotes very little space to consideration of the status of 'what happens for the most part'; and it must remain uncertain to what extent he would have been able to distinguish the objectively probable from what most people believe will happen. That is to say, it is not clear that he envisaged a situation in which there could be a probability of something's happening although this probability was not recognised by the majority of people.[63] But even if we regard this as an open question, in *An. Pr.* B27 it is the word '*eikos*' rather than '*endoxos*' which expresses the notion of probability. If the two words were equivalent in meaning, Aristotle's comment that an *eikos* is an endoxic premiss would have no explanatory force. When he also says here that the *eikos* is what *they* know to happen for the most part, this further suggests that Aristotle uses '*endoxos*' here to indicate a reference to people's views. The evidence, then, for a sense of '*endoxos*' in which it means 'objectively probable' is slender. If we take the basic sense of the word as 'representative of someone's view', as we shall find it to be in other passages, we can interpret its occurrence in *An. Pr.* B27 as an extension of this. But it would not be possible to regard 'representative of someone's view' as an extension of a more basic sense of 'objectively probable', since such probabilities exist independently of the views which people may hold about them.

It has been necessary to devote some attention to this interpretation of the meaning of '*endoxos*' because of the influence which *An. Pr.* B27 has exerted on interpreters of the *Topics*. But in the

---

[60] *Logique Et Méthode Chez Aristote*, pp. 9–16.

[61] 70a2–6.

[62] 70a6–7.

[63] Compare the converse view (*An. Post.* A30; *Met.* E2, 1027a20–6) that what is improbable cannot be studied.

Topics itself there is no passage in which one is inclined to interpret the word in this way, and the main discussions of the notion tell against this interpretation. At *Top.* A1, 100b21–3, endoxic premisses are characterised as ones which 'seem to all or to most or to the savants (*sophoi*), and of these either to all or to most or to the most understanding (*gnōrimoi*) and view-holding (*endoxoi*)'.[64] This characterisation is repeated at the beginning of the discussion of dialectical questions in *Top.* A10.[65] There, however, Aristotle adds the qualification that the question must not be paradoxical; for a question which represents a view of the savants will not find acceptance if this view conflicts with the views of the many.[66] Examples of such paradoxical views are Antisthenes' view that contradiction is impossible or Heraclitus' view that everything is in motion; and they have their place in dialectic, but as *theses* – starting-points to be defended against the questioner,[67] not as questions to be used in the attack and defence of the starting-points.[68] It is, of course, essential that paradoxical views should not be totally debarred from dialectic, since they form an important part of the *aporiai* which must be examined as a preliminary to the construction of a science and which essentially fall within the province of dialectic. But it is important to use them carefully within the dialectical exercise.

A number of other important points are made in *Top.* A10–11 about the sorts of endoxic statement which may be used in dialectic. A question which everyone would agree in answering in the affirmative or negative cannot be allowed to be dialectical,[69] nor can such questions as 'should we honour the gods or not' or 'is snow white or not?'.[70] Dialectical questions are concerned with matters about which there is difficulty and dispute; and questions to which all would agree the answer clearly do not belong to this class, while questions of the second rejected type are such, Aristotle maintains, as to be answered by punishment or the use of the senses and not by argument. It is the presence of an argument to support them or of a reputation for philosophical skill on the part of their proponents, which justifies the admission to dialectic of the paradoxical

---

[64] I construe '*endoxos*', used of a man, as paronymously related to '*endoxon*', as I have argued (p. 68, n. 28 above) '*gnōrimos*' to be related to *gnōrimon*'. The present passage confirms the earlier claim. Note that there are very few contexts in which '*endoxos*' is used of a man.

[65] 104a8–10.

[66] 104a10–12.

[67] That this is what Aristotle means by '*thesis*' in the context of dialectic is clear from *Top.* Θ3, 159a3–6, where the original position is distinguished from points subsequently introduced to defend it; cf. Waitz, *Organon* vol. 2, *ad loc.* and also on *An. Post.* 72a15.

[68] *Top.* A11, 104b18–28.

[69] 104a4–8.

[70] 105a3–9.

theses;[71] and Aristotle is quite ready to admit as dialectical questions those which contain the views of experts in various skills.[72] Generally, Aristotle maintains that dialectic must concern itself with matters where there is *aporia*, the difficulty being caused either by the existence of conflicting arguments about the particular problem or by the lack of a satisfactory explanation of the matter.[73]

Nevertheless some problems remain after the discussion in *Top.* A10–11. Firstly, there seems to be an inconsistency when Aristotle says *both* that matters which are universally agreed cannot form the subject-matter of dialectic[74] *and* that a question which is endoxic *to all* may be dialectical.[75] Secondly, despite what was said above about the position of the paradox in dialectic, we may still feel some doubt about the ban on offering paradoxes as dialectical questions which Aristotle imposes at 104a10–12. The discussion of *endoxa* in *Top.* Θ5 throws light on both these points. In this chapter Aristotle is concerned with the strategy which should be adopted by the answerer in dialectical exercises which are conducted not in a contentious spirit but for the sake of testing and examining the views on some question.[76] He has already said that the aim of the questioner is 'so to lead the argument on as to make the answerer say the most implausible (*adoxon*) of the things that follow necessarily from the thesis', and that of the answerer is 'that the impossibility or paradox should seem to follow not through him but through the thesis'.[77] In Θ5 he expands this advice. He argues that whatever is *endoxon* or *adoxon* may be so either without qualification or in a way which is qualified by reference to some person: this person may be the defender of the thesis or someone else.[78] If the thesis which the answerer is upholding is *endoxon*, the questioner must prove a conclusion which is *adoxon*, and vice versa;[79] and the qualification or lack of it which attaches to the answerer's *endoxon*

[71] 104b19–28.

[72] 104a15, 33–7.

[73] 104b12–17: '[dialectical] problems are both those for which there are pieces of contrary reasoning (the difficulty is whether it is so or not, because there are persuasive arguments on both sides), and those about which we do not have an argument, since they are important and we find it hard to present the explanation'; *Rhet.* A2, 1356b37: '[dialectic reasons] from what needs argument'.

[74] 104a4–8, 104b3–5.

[75] 100b21, 104a9.

[76] 159a25–37. This passage is important both for the originality which Aristotle claims for his treatment of the non-contentious form of dialectic and as evidence against those commentators who do not recognise a distinction between serious dialectic and contentious eristic. For a strong argument for the importance of this distinction, see G. E. L. Owen, 'Dialectic and Eristic in the Treatment of the Forms', pp. 103–7.

[77] Θ4, 159a18–22.   [78] 159a39–159b1.   [79] 159b4–6.

must similarly attach to the questioner's *adoxon*.[80] In serious dialectic it is important to be clear about whose views, if indeed they are those of any particular person, are being examined. Accordingly Aristotle requires that the examination of a thesis of, for example, Heraclitus should not ignore the fact that it is Heraclitus' view which is under discussion: the answerer must not allow that something is *endoxon* unless it accords with the views of Heraclitus, and in doing this he is allowed the licence of imagining what the author of the particular thesis *would* say as well as being required to reproduce what he actually does say.[81] It is interesting to find Aristotle requiring of the serious dialectician this fidelity in representing the views of others, because the quality of Aristotle's *practice* in the dialectical examinations of the views of his predecessors and contemporaries, which he conducts so frequently in his works, is of immense importance to the historian of earlier Greek philosophy. W. K. C. Guthrie has argued against Cherniss and J. B. McDiarmid that Aristotle shows a sound historical sense when he comments on the views of the Presocratics;[82] and we would expect Aristotle's practice to show this if he is following the recommendations which he makes in *Top.* Θ5.

The value of the requirement that we should consistently maintain the qualifications which attach to an *endoxon*, i.e. that we should not forget *whose* view is being examined, is clear. When Plato and Aristotle argue against Heraclitus' theory of constant flux that it entails the impossibility of Heraclitus' own thesis being true,[83] their procedure is consistent with the recommendation of *Top.* Θ5: they use Heraclitus' own views to argue for a view which Heraclitus would not wish to accept, that is, they start from a qualified *endoxon* and argue for a qualified *adoxon*. But if the notion of the qualified *endoxon* is clear, that of the unqualified *endoxon* is less so. Alexander argues that Aristotle means the views of everyone or of the majority when he speaks of unqualified *endoxa*: these do not need to be qualified as do those of some particular person.[84] Alexander's suggestion is plausible both because Aristotle does allow such *endoxa* as dialectical in *Top.* A1 and A10 and because in other contexts Aristotle clearly intends to indicate this type of universality when he speaks of the unqualifiedly such-and-such. Thus at *De Caelo* Δ4, 311a15–29, the unqualifiedly weighty is that which sinks

---

[80] 159b16–17, 25–9.

[81] 159b27–35.

[82] 'Aristotle as a Historian of Philosophy'; *A History Of Greek Philosophy*, vol. 1, pp. 41–3.

[83] Plato *Theaet.* 183a–183b; Aristotle *Met.* Γ8, 1012b13–18. These are examples of what J. L. Mackie, 'Self-Refutation – A Formal Analysis', pp. 196–7, calls 'operational' self-refutation.

[84] *In Topica* 549.22–5.

beneath *everything,* and it is contrasted with that which sinks beneath only some things and is therefore not weighty *without qualification.* But I have already argued[85] that in a number of cases where Aristotle finds it valuable to distinguish between the absolute and the qualified forms of a concept the type of universality which he regards as attaching to the concept in its absolute form is different from that which in the *De Caelo* attaches to the absolute heavy. One of these cases is the concept of intelligibility, as is clear from the suggestion at *Top.* Z4, 142a9–10, that the absolutely intelligible may not be intelligible to everyone. Since the notion of being more intelligible plays a prominent part in the discussion of *endoxa* in *Top.* Θ5,[86] it would be reasonable to expect that a similar complexity attaches to the concept of *endoxon* as attaches to the concepts of intelligibility and the object of wish which also are applied both with and without qualification.

Unfortunately, in the absence of a discussion of the conflict of views which can be resolved by using the distinction between the qualified and the unqualified uses of the expression, it is not possible to prove that the distinction has the same force in the case of the concept of the endoxic as it has in the case of those concepts about which there is such a conflict of views. Nevertheless, I should argue that it is wrong to reduce 'the unqualifiedly endoxic' to 'the view of any particular person or group of people', which Alexander does when he interprets it as 'the views of all or of the majority'. I have noted that there is a difficulty in allowing that a view which *everybody* shares can have a place in dialectic, since dialectic is essentially concerned with matters about which there is difficulty and conflict of views.[87] A view which is universally accepted could not form a subject for dialectical debate; and yet it is precisely the endoxic character of various subjects of dialectical debate which Aristotle discusses in *Top.* Θ5. Aristotle frequently speaks of questions on which there is conflict between the views of the savants and the ordinary mass of people.[88] But it is not clear that the views of the savants have any less claim to be called views *simpliciter* than do those of the mass, particularly in view of the fact that Aristotle readily allows that the views of experts in the various skills can be produced as dialectical questions.[89] The second difficulty which I noticed as arising from the discussion of *Top.* A10–11 is that it

[85] pp. 64–7 above.
[86] 159b8–15 – the premisses must be more endoxic and more intelligible than the conclusion.
[87] p. 80 above.
[88] *Top.* A11, 104b4–5; *SE* 12, 173a22–3.
[89] *Top.* A10, 104a14–15. At *EE* A3, 1215a1–4, Aristotle says that only the savants' views on happiness need be considered: the views of the mass can be ignored, since the latter is insufficiently experienced in reasoning.

might be thought that the ban on presenting the paradoxical views of the savants, except as initial theses, is unreasonable; for it seems to preclude the sort of *ad hominem* examination which is recommended in *Top*. Θ5, 159b25–35, where the particular authorship of the views from which the examination starts is not ignored in the examination itself. However, if we interpret 'unqualifiedly *endoxon*' as meaning 'plausible' and '*endoxon* for so-and-so' as meaning 'the view of some particular person',[90] these difficulties can be resolved. As for the second, something may be a paradox, despite the fact that it is the view of someone and not paradoxical *to him*. But in case this be thought to make the notion of paradox dependent on the views of all or the majority, it must be stressed that the view of the many may not be plausible because of difficulties which are appreciated only by a few experts. Light is also thrown on the first difficulty when we realise that it is not the same thing to be a view which is held by everyone or by the majority and to be unconditionally plausible. If the plausibility of the view is to be established unconditionally, an examination must be conducted which will confirm everyone or the majority as having *justification* for accepting this view. So a view which is endoxic to all or to the majority may still not be unqualifiedly endoxic, if there is reason for doubting its ability to survive examination; and it may, therefore, be suitable for inclusion within the conduct of the dialectical exercise.

I am not suggesting that Aristotle is attempting with his notion of the unqualifiedly endoxic to divorce the notion of plausibility from the subjects – the people and groups who have their own views – to whom it is essentially related. Rather, I maintain that with this notion he is attempting to allow for a distinction between the area of dialectical debate in which we recognise the distinct authorship of the various views and adhere to the limitations which this imposes on the discussion, and the area where we are concerned with the absolute plausibility of the thesis under discussion. Both forms of debate have their value. I have already commented on the value of considering a thesis in terms of what its author would accept rather than in terms of what someone else might accept.[91] But it is equally important, if not more so, to discover whether a thesis is acceptable *at all*; and to do this we must go beyond the views of any particular person and consider the absolute plausibility, unqualified by reference to this person, of his thesis by examining its consequences. At *SE* 3, 165b14, Aristotle says that it is one of the five aims of the eristic disputant to force the answerer to say something paradoxical; and there is nothing to suggest that this aim, like the other four

90 There is no reason why the 'definedly endoxic' should be defined by reference to an individual rather than a group of people.
91 p. 81 above.

there mentioned, is not also shared by serious dialectic. When he discusses the attempts to produce paradox in *SE* 12, he says that one of the means used by the eristic questioner is to play off the views of the many against those of the savants; and he recommends that we combat this tactic by showing that we have not been forced to utter the paradox because of *the questioner's own argument*.[92] From this we may infer that Aristotle regarded it as genuinely reprehensible that one should be forced by proper means to utter a paradox. The same idea is to be seen at *Top.* Θ4, 159a22-4, when he follows his comment that the answerer must attempt to show that any paradox which he may utter is forced on him by the position which he has undertaken to defend, with the words 'for there may be a distinction between the errors of *positing the wrong thing in the first place* and, having posited it, of not protecting it properly'. Although we should recognise that paradoxical consequences are liable to arise from a paradoxical thesis and that the fact that the thesis is paradoxical lessens the blame which attaches to the uttering of these paradoxical consequences, the uttering of paradox at any stage is ultimately unacceptable.

In the discussion of topics in the body of the *Topics* Aristotle frequently appeals to *what seems to be so*. This category is worked into the discussion most systematically in the treatment of the *a fortiori* arguments, as is particularly clear at *Top.* B10, 115a6-14. Here Aristotle presents a number of topics, of which the following is typical: 'if that which *has the greater appearance* of being an attribute of the subject is not in fact an attribute of it, nor will that which *has the lesser appearance* of being an attribute be one'.[93] When Aristotle speaks in these, and many other passages of the *Topics*, of what seems to be so, there is no indication of any specific reference for the views to which he appeals. The *a fortiori* arguments are presented in terms of the absolutely plausible. This does not exclude the possibility of their being applied to situations in which the relatively plausible is being examined: here the discussion would be confined to what is or would be acceptable or unacceptable to some particular person. Nevertheless, these are no more than applications of a general rule about what is plausible. The general rule is concerned with the concept of the plausible; and this is indeed related to subjects but not any *particular* subject.

It is possible, if we remember the conflict of views which precedes

---

[92] 172b29-35.

[93] 115a8-10. The mention of *seeming* in the *a fortiori* topics of *Top.* B10 is striking when one compares them with the related topics of *Top.* E8 and H3; *Top.* Δ6, 127b26-7, makes it clear, as does *Top.* B10, that in *a fortiori* arguments the variation of degree essentially relates to the readiness of people to accept one attribution more readily than another.

Aristotle's use of the distinction between the absolute and the relative to analyse the object of wish and the object of understanding, to reconstruct the sort of difficulty which may have prompted him to distinguish the absolutely from the relatively plausible. On the one hand there is the relativist: he recognises that to be plausible is essentially to be plausible to someone, but goes to the extreme of reducing the notion of plausibility to that of being someone's view. This makes it impossible for him to compare the views which are held, in respect of their plausibility. On the other hand there is the realist, who recognises that to be plausible is not to be plausible to any given person; but his treatment of the plausible errs in ignoring the particular authorship of the views which are actually held. Aristotle steers his way between these two extremes. He is a realist to the extent of recognising that there are some views – those which are propounded by the man who fails to use his senses or needs punishment – which do not need to be considered because of their absolute implausibility. He further agrees with the realist in recognising the concept of absolute plausibility, and in recognising that this concept is essential to dialectic insofar as the final aim in dialectic is to force one's opponent to say something as implausible (absolutely) as possible.[94] But he agrees with the relativist in recognising the need to start from the views which are already available and to observe carefully, as we examine them, the peculiar character of each.

The plausible, like the object of wish and the other concepts that we have been examining in this review of Aristotle's metaphysical theory, can take an absolute form: in this form it is not defined by reference to any given person or group. But the way for us to approach it is through an examination of the relative forms which it also assumes. Only by studying the actual reactions of subjects, the ways in which people's faculties are actually exercised on their objects, can we sift the better from the worse exercises of the faculty; and this is how we can come to realise how the faculty and its object ought to be related.

The nature of the discussion of ethics

This leads us to a further aspect of Aristotle's metaphysical theory, the dynamic one which examines how progress occurs in ethical and intellectual matters. He uses the distinction between the qualified and unqualified forms of concepts to illuminate this. I shall argue that the metaphysical analysis is important to a proper understanding of what he says about the nature of his enterprise in the works

[94] *Top.* Θ4, 159a18–20.

on ethics and dialectic: moreover, when the purpose of these works is grasped, the static analysis of their central concepts which has been given above is confirmed.

In *EN* A3 and B2 Aristotle makes a number of important points about the method to be pursued in a work of the type on which he is embarking. Firstly, he warns us against expecting that the discussion of ethical problems will be characterised by the degree of precision (*akribeia*) that is to be expected in other forms of discussion.[95] The notion of precision which Aristotle appeals to here is one by which greater precision is a function of being more simple and less in need of support from a number of additional items. This is clear from *Met.* A2, 982a25–8, where he says: 'most precise among the sciences are those especially that treat primary things; for those which are built from fewer things are more precise than those where the definitions involve additional items, as is arithmetic than geometry'. The contrast between the greater precision of the sciences which deal with the elementary, and the lesser precision of those which deal with the complexes built up from these elements by extension,[96] is in turn connected with the distinction between the unqualified and the qualified. The link between the precise and the simple is clear from *Met.* M3, 1078a9–11, – 'the more it is concerned with things which are prior in definition and more simple, the more precise it is (this is what simplicity is)'. Two further texts clearly bring out the connection between the qualified and the complex. At *EN* H4, 1148a10–11, Aristotle contrasts the incontinent man 'said without qualification' and 'said by addition'; and at *Met.* Z4, 1030a28–34, he contrasts substances, which have essences without qualification, with things in other categories, which have essences only by extension or abstraction.[97] In both cases Aristotle intends by this contrast to distinguish the case in which the name applies without any need of further explanation, with the case in which such explanation and qualification is necessary.

Aristotle's reason for saying that precision beyond a certain degree is not to be expected in ethics is that (a) any general account is bound to obscure the variations in obligation that arise from the varieties of circumstance attending the performance of any action,[98] while (b) the particular account will have to be so hedged with qualifications if it is to fit the particular case (as the general account does not), that it will inevitably lack the simplicity which Aristotle regards as characteristic of precision.[99] This does not mean that there is not in each set of circumstances a right answer to the ques-

[95] 1094b11–27; 1103b34–1104a10.
[96] See also *An. Post.* A27, 87a31–7.
[97] 1030a33: 'adding and subtracting'.
[98] 1094b14–19.   [99] 1104a5–10.

tion of how one should act. Aristotle is convinced that there is a right answer, and that this is achieved by the man who exercises *phronēsis* and acts in accordance with the right reason.[100] But in a work which treats generally of ethics the discussion cannot fully reflect the complexity of the particular cases; and accordingly Aristotle says that the account which he will present in the *Nicomachean Ethics* can only be a rough and outline account.

Two further features of Aristotle's conception of method in the treatment of ethics are important. Firstly, he insists that his purpose is unlike that of a theoretical investigation. In a practical subject such as ethics the aim is not to *know* but to *do*;[101] and his discussion is not intended to instruct us on the nature of virtue, but to show us how to live well. Secondly, the audience at which Aristotle's discussion is aimed is limited in number. There must be some disposition to listen to reason in matters of conduct, and this excludes from the number of those capable of benefiting from Aristotle's discussion the young, who are excessively dominated by emotion and inexperienced in life, and others, young not in years but in character, who also allow excessive play to their emotions.[102] Aristotle justifies this second point at *EN* A4, 1095b2–13, by saying that we must start from what we understand and move towards what is absolutely intelligible: so in ethics the student must have a character such that he has a correct view of the moral truth, in order that then he can be brought to an appreciation of the reasons for its being the truth.

I should argue that there is a close connection between these comments on the nature of a work on ethics and the analysis of certain central ethical concepts for which Aristotle uses the distinction between the unqualified and the qualified. At *EN* E1, 1129b4–6, after distinguishing the simply good from what is good for someone, he says 'men pray for and pursue the former, but this is wrong; they should pray that things good without qualification should be good also for them, but should choose things good for them'. It is no accident that Aristotle's comment here on the effect which the distinction between the unqualified and the qualified good should have on our manner of conduct, accords so well with his comment on the effect which the same distinction between intelligibles should have on our manner of learning. For we have already seen that the distinction is put to the same use, and resolves the same sorts of problems, in the case of both concepts. We must start from where we already are – from what we find good and from what we understand – if we wish to advance to the chosen territory of the absolutely good and the absolutely intelligible. The absolutely good is

[100] 1103b32, 1144a6–9, 1144b21–8.
[101] 1103b26–31.   [102] 1095a2–13.

that which is found to be good by the man who sees the truth in moral matters. The object of his wish is what we must focus attention on if we are to get the right answer to moral problems. But because Aristotle's aim in ethics is to instruct people on how to live, he cannot ignore the various objects of actual wishes; and this means that he cannot concentrate exclusively on the absolute and unqualified objects of the various faculties. I argued above that one of the applications of the distinction between the unqualified and the qualified is to mark the distinction between the simple and the complex, and that this distinction in turn is connected with that between more and less precise forms of enquiry. In *EN* A3 and B2 the treatment of ethics is said to lack precision; and in terms of the distinction between the unqualified and the qualified forms of a concept, this will mean that the writer on ethics will have to concern himself with instances in which the concept is qualified as well as with the concept in its absolute form, which is the form in which it is conceived by the moral expert. This is as one would expect, in view of Aristotle's belief that in order to instruct people on how to live well one must start from what *they* understand and, from this basis, produce in them an understanding of what is intelligible in an unqualified way.

It follows that the analysis which Aristotle provides of such concepts as the object of wish, pleasure, the object of friendship, has an importance which goes beyond the solution of problems associated with these particular concepts. This analysis follows the sort of pattern which we should expect from Aristotle's general comments on the nature of ethical philosophy; and to understand this is valuable for our general understanding of what Aristotle is about in his works on ethics. Here, once again, Aristotle's position should be represented as a *via media* which avoids two undesirable extremes. On the one hand, there is the extreme realist view of ethics, which would require that concepts should be considered only in their absolute form. This view would demand that the writer on ethics should ignore, as irrelevant to a work on how to live well, the qualified forms in which these concepts are understood by those whose lives are less than completely satisfactory. On the other hand, there is the extreme relativist view, which would require that the writer on ethics should make no attempt to discriminate between the completely satisfactory life and that which fails to come up to this standard. Aristotle avoids both these extremes;[103] and this is a feature not only of his analysis of certain particular concepts in

---

[103] For an indication of Aristotle's opposition to both these views, compare the discussion of Socrates' dictum that no-one does wrong knowingly (*EN* Γ5, 1113b3–14), where it is objected that since this leaves no room for assigning blame to actions, it also leaves no room for assigning praise.

ethics but of his whole conception of the manner in which a treatise on ethics should be executed.

The nature of the discussion of dialectic

Aristotle's comments on the character of his treatment of dialectic in the *Topics* bear a considerable similarity to his comments on his treatment of ethics in the *Nicomachean Ethics*. At *Top.* A1, 101a18–24, he says that his aim in writing a work on dialectic is not to give a precise account but only to provide an outline description of the various matters which he will treat, since this is sufficient for a work of this character. The similarity between this comment on the treatment of dialectic and the comments on the treatment of ethics is striking. In both cases Aristotle says that he will avoid the precise account,[104] and elects to provide an outline account,[105] as is demanded by the nature of the subject matter. A difference between the comments in the two works is that in the *Topics* there is no discussion, as there is in the *Nicomachean Ethics*, of the reasons why the account should be only an outline one. There is no mention in *Top.* A1 of such considerations as the variety of circumstances which arise in the exercise of the art of dialectic, considerations to which Aristotle appeals in *EN* A3 and B2 to support his comments on the treatment of ethical problems. Nevertheless I believe that it can be shown that the same sort of considerations underlie these comments in both works. But first I want to examine in more detail the similarities between Aristotle's general comments on the treatment of dialectic and those on the treatment of ethics.

In a number of further passages in the *Topics* Aristotle repeats the comment of *Top.* A1 that precision beyond a certain degree is not to be expected in a work on dialectic. At *Top.* H3, 153a11–15, he says about the ensuing discussion on the means of establishing a definition: 'It falls to another enterprise to explain *with precision* both what a definition is and how one should define; *but now it suffices for our present need* to say just that there can be reasoning for a definition and essence.' In a similar vein are those passages in the *Topics* and the *Analytics* which describe the treatment of a question in the work on dialectic as 'in accordance with opinion' and the corresponding treatment in the work on the syllogism as 'in accordance with truth'. We find a striking case of a pair of passages from different works which use this distinction to cross-refer to each other: a remark at *Top.* Θ13, 162b31–3, that the nature of question-begging argument 'has been stated in the *Analytics* according to truth, and is now to be stated according to opinion', is

---

[104] *Top.* A1, 101a21; *EN* A3, 1094b13.
[105] *Top.* A1, 101a22; *EN* B2, 1104a1.

answered at *An. Pr.* B16, 65a35–7, with 'begging the point at issue is, in demonstrations, when things are so in truth, but in dialectical affairs when they are so in opinion'. The reasons for drawing this distinction vary according to context.[106] Thus in *Top.* Θ13 the treatment is described as 'in accordance with opinion' because he intends to examine the ways in which someone might *be taken to* beg the question. The language of the chapter[107] shows that Aristotle's concern here is as much with whether the question is judged to be begged as with whether it actually is begged; but in *An. Pr.* B16 there is no mention of these potentially subjective considerations. Elsewhere, as in *An. Pr.* A30 and *An. Post.* A19, the dialectical treatment of a question is described as 'in accordance with opinion' because the premisses from which dialectical reasoning works represent no more than views.

But although Aristotle's reasons for designating the dialectical treatment in this way vary in different contexts, the general character of the contrast between the treatment of a question in accordance with opinion and with truth is the same. He is contrasting the treatment which is concerned with the truth of the matter, with the treatment which is concerned rather with the ways in which people are prepared to accept some account of the matter. The need to pay attention to the reactions of people and not simply to the question itself inevitably lessens the universal and absolute character of what can be said, since it requires that we should take account of the differences in reaction which may be exhibited by the various people. This point has been fully discussed: its importance here is that the contrast which Aristotle draws between the treatments in accordance with opinion and with truth throws light on his comments in *Top.* A1 about the imprecise character of the discussion of dialectic which is to follow. I have argued that in the *Nicomachean Ethics* Aristotle's reason for saying that the treatment will not be precise is that the variety of circumstances which must be considered when we determine how to act in each particular case make it impossible to give a general account which is not hedged with qualifications. In dialectic also we find the same variety of circumstances and the same need to appreciate that any general comments that may be made on the practice of dialectic will need to be qualified by reference to the particular circumstances of that practice.

We saw that it was an important feature of Aristotle's view of his treatment of ethics that he conceived his aim as the production not of knowledge of how one should act but of correct action, and that

---

[106] Further instances are supplied by *Top.* A14, 105b30–1; *An. Pr.* A30, 46a8–10; *An. Post.* A19, 81b18–23.

[107] Especially at 162b34–6, 163a4–7.

connected with this was his belief that the audience which can benefit from his discussion is necessarily limited to those who start with a suitable moral disposition.[108] Similar views to these are to be found in Aristotle's comments on dialectic. In *Top.* A3 he compares dialectic with rhetoric and medicine, and says that in the case of all three faculties the possession of skill is marked by the ability to work successfully with *suitable* materials: not all materials are suitable, and it is not required of the man who exercises these faculties that he should be able to achieve success with just any materials. The same point is made about rhetoric at *Rhet.* A1, 1355b10–14, where the comparison with medicine is once again introduced. Rhetoric is limited in the possibility of what it can achieve, and we cannot require that the man who possesses the skill should be persuasive in all circumstances. It is sufficient that he should do what can be done with the materials available, just as it is possible for the doctor to show his skill with the incurable even though he cannot cure them.

In a number of passages in the *Topics* Aristotle shows how the dialectician should pay attention to the materials with which he works. At *Top.* A12, 105a16–19, and Θ2, 157a18–21, he recommends the use of induction against the many and of syllogism against the expert in dialectic. At *Top.* Θ14, 164a12–164b7, he distinguishes the various procedures one should follow in gymnastic dialectic according to the age and experience of one's opponent, and goes on to justify the distinction by reference to the general aims of this form of dialectic; and at *Top.* Θ14, 164b8–15, he warns those who seek to be trained in dialectic to avoid chance dialectical encounters, on the grounds that these are likely to be conducted in a contentious spirit and be unsatisfactory as pieces of argument.[109] All these passages, then, provide instances in which the dialectician is recommended to pay attention to the character of his opponent. Another way in which the dialectician should recognise qualifications which must be imposed on the purely logical character of the reasoning by circumstances external to it, is discussed in *Top.* Θ11, 161b34–162a8. Here Aristotle argues that when one assigns praise or blame to an argument one should pay attention not only to the argument itself but also to the nature of the problem with which it is concerned. The fact that problems can be easier or more difficult means that an argument which would in itself be censurable may nevertheless be

---

[108] For a further indication of the connection between these two beliefs, cf. *EN* K9, 1179a35–1179b16, where Aristotle says that the aim in ethics is the production of correct living, and that while a limited number of naturally gifted men will be stimulated to this by argument, with the majority argument is useless and some other means must be found.

[109] cf. 164b13, and Θ5, 159a25–36, discussed on pp. 80–1 above.

laudable in view of the difficulty of the problem; and *vice versa* the argument may be in itself laudable, but censurable in view of the fact that there are clearer means of proof available. It is striking that Aristotle says of the proofs of the more difficult problems 'if he wrests his conclusion from premises which are as endoxic as possible, his dialectic is good'.[110] This comment recalls the general remark of *Top.* A3 that dialectical skill consists in doing one's best with the available materials. In *Top.* Θ11 we see a clear application of this general principle. So these are two ways in which we may have to qualify the absolute character of the dialectical argument – by reference to the other people involved in the dialectical exercise, or to the nature of the problem with which we are dealing.

I argued that in Aristotle's general comments on the character of his treatment of ethical problems there is a connection between the three features: the description of the treatment as imprecise, the requirement that the audience be naturally gifted, and the insistence that his aim is to produce correct action and not theoretical knowledge. I should similarly argue that there is a connection between these three features in his comments on the treatment of dialectic, although less space is devoted to methodological discussion in the *Topics* than in the *Nicomachean Ethics* and so both these features themselves and the connection between them are less clear in the former work. Aristotle is aware that the conditions of the exercise of dialectical skill are such that, although the dialectician is indeed required to argue his case by purely logical means,[111] he must at the same time not ignore the various ways in which circumstances which are external to his argument can affect its character. In dialectic one is required to convince, by logical means, actual people of the truth of some particular assertion. This is not the same as the ideal of pure logic, which is to free the conditions of proof from dependence on the variations which may be imposed by the audience or the problems treated. Dialectic must be sensitive to these variations; and the work which seeks to produce dialectical skill in its audience is inevitably reduced in its precision because the situations with which it is concerned may be qualified by these variations.

We have seen that Aristotle analyses such central concepts of dialectic as the intelligible and the endoxic in a way which parallels his analysis of the object of wish and other central ethical concepts. Moreover this latter analysis conforms with his theory of method in ethics: as we read at *EN* E1, 1129b4–6, we must choose what is

---

[110] 161b37–8.

[111] cf. the prohibition at *Top.* B5, 112a7–11, on introducing into one's argument matters which are logically irrelevant. Further texts which tell in the same direction are considered by G. E. L. Owen in 'Dialectic and Eristic in the Treatment of the Forms', p. 107.

NATURE OF THE DISCUSSION OF DIALECTIC

good for us and pray that this may also be good without qualification. He goes on to draw a parallel between intellectual and moral progress at *Met.* Z3, 1029b5–8: 'the task is, as in the case of actions to make out of what is good for each man the completely good good for each man, so to make out of what is more intelligible to him the naturally more intelligible more intelligible to him'. Just as in ethics if we must proceed from the qualified to the unqualified good, this necessarily lessens the precision which a treatment of the matter can possess, so also in dialectic the nature of the concepts which are to be treated lessens the precision which Aristotle's discussion can possess. Commentators have sometimes understood Aristotle's references to the fact that the treatment in the *Topics* is imprecise or 'in accordance with opinion' as meaning that the *Topics* presents an *unnecessarily* rough account of matters which are in principle treatable in a less slovenly way and which are so treated in the *Analytics*. Thus Cherniss says of *Top.* H3, which refers the reader to a work other than the *Topics* for a 'precise' investigation of definition, that 'the stress put upon the necessity of assumption and the respondent's consent rather implies that a strict examination would show such demonstration to be impossible'.[112] Cherniss supposes that the 'strict examination' is to be found in the *Posterior Analytics*. Against this I should argue that the *Topics* and the *Posterior Analytics* are concerned with different, though related, questions. If the treatment in the *Topics* is less precise than the related discussion in the *Posterior Analytics*,[113] this is because in the *Topics* Aristotle is concerned with such concepts as intelligibility not only in their absolute form, as he is in the *Analytics*, but also in their qualified form, as he is not in the *Analytics*. In the *Topics* he *elects* to treat these concepts in their full complexity; and it is for this reason that the treatment in the *Topics* is imprecise.

But the imprecision is not something which it would be desirable to eliminate. As is clear from *Met.* Z3, 1029b3–12, intellectual advance occurs when, starting from what we find intelligible, we come to find intelligible that which is so without qualification. This means that the discussion of the technique by which intellectual advance is produced must recognise intelligibility in both of its forms, the qualified as well as the unqualified; and since dialectic is this technique,[114] recognition of these two forms of intelligibility is essential in dialectic. That this means that the treatment of dialectic

---

[112] *Aristotle's Criticism of Plato and the Academy*, vol. i, p. 34 n. 28.
[113] Cherniss' identification of the reference should be accepted. He follows Solmsen (*Die Entwicklung der aristotelischen Logik und Rhetorik*, p. 151 n. 2), who argues against the attempt of Maier (*Die Syllogistik des Aristoteles*, ii, pt. 2, p. 78 n. 3) to argue that the reference is to *Top.* Z.
[114] cf. *Top.* A2, 101a34–101b4, and the discussion on pp. 31–52 above.

will be imprecise does not impair the value of the treatment. As in ethics so also in dialectic there is a right procedure in each instance; but in both cases the general account cannot fully reflect the complexity of the particular circumstances and cannot, therefore, be more than a rough and outline guide. But to attempt to represent the *Topics* as an unsuccessful exercise in pure logic, i.e. as a first draft on the *Analytics*, or again as a manual of instruction on how to win a debate at all costs, is to make the same sort of mistake as occurs when people attempt to identify the object of wish either with the good or with the apparent good. In the case of the object of wish each of the identifications, though not altogether unhelpful, nevertheless represents an attempt to reduce the concept to another concept which is related to it but distinct from it. Similarly, the attempts to interpret Aristotle's discussion of dialectic in the *Topics*, which have so dominated modern commentary on the work, as if it were concerned *solely* with the argument itself or *solely* with the reactions of people to the argument represent attempts to reduce the work to another type of enterprise from which it is essentially distinct. The *Topics* is *sui generis*. Its purpose and character is different from that of the other Aristotelian works with which it has been so readily compared.

Platonic metaphysics: Topics Z8 and Parmenides 133–134

All through this exploration of Aristotle's metaphysical theory we have not mentioned Plato. Yet his views on the relation between faculties and their objects are an essential ingredient in the inheritance of problems which Aristotle's theory seeks to resolve. They also play a crucial part in Plato's own favoured metaphysical theory, the theory of Forms. Earlier in this study I compared the two philosophers' ideas on the relation between dialectic and other intellectual enterprise; I maintained that the differences in these ideas are not to be minimised and that they reflect deep differences in ontological theory. Now that we have examined Aristotle's metaphysical theory on which his ideas about the intellectual enterprises are based, we must do the same for its Platonic precursor, albeit more briefly. This will complete the review of the theoretical basis of Aristotelian dialectic.

In one of the topics which Aristotle says can be used against those who maintain the theory of Forms, he exploits the distinction between the real and the apparent.[115] The first part of the topic notes that when we define an appetite (*orexis*), we must mention the *appearance* of that towards which it is directed. Thus, the definition of *wish* as 'appetite for the good' is open to the objection that the

[115] *Top.* Z8, 146b36–147a11.

appetites of the various individuals who exercise a wish are not necessarily directed towards the good but only towards what seems good to them.[116] The second part of the topic shows how this consideration can be turned against one who maintains the theory of Forms. If he accepts that the definition should mention appearance, then it is possible to use the Platonic *endoxon* that Forms are correlative with Forms to show that his admission entails that there is a Form of the Apparent Good. However, in their metaphysics the Platonists make a radical distinction between the apparent and the real; and since they would regard the object of definition as the Form, and Forms are correlative with each other, their acceptance of the need to mention appearance in the definition is inconsistent with their metaphysics.[117]

Little attention has been devoted by the commentators to this argument; and of those who have noticed it, the majority have not regarded it as revealing a serious difficulty in the theory of Forms.[118] An exception is G. E. L. Owen,[119] who argues that Plato's view of the Forms as standard samples provides Aristotle with his justification for maintaining here that the Platonist could not allow that there is a Form of the Apparent Good, since something which has a character only *apparently*, and not *really*, cannot serve as a standard sample of that character. But the argument gains in importance when it is considered in the light of the Aristotelian analyses of central ethical and dialectical concepts which we have been examining; and this aspect of it has largely been ignored by others.

Although Aristotle's examples of the way in which the topic may be used both use proposed definitions of appetites, the topic may be applied in all the cases where Aristotle uses the distinction between the qualified and unqualified forms of a concept to analyse the relation between a faculty and its objects.[120] In requiring that the definition of *wish* should mention the *apparent* good, he is making the same point as that which he makes against the extreme realist in *EN* Γ4: a particular exercise of the faculty of wish is no less real as an act of wish for being directed towards that which is not the real object of the faculty.[121] We saw that the extreme realist's view that all acts of wishing are necessarily directed towards the object

[116] 146b36–147a5.
[117] 147a5–11.
[118] Cherniss, *Aristotle's Criticism of Plato and the Academy*, vol. 1, p. 8, p. 282 n. 189. During, 'Aristotle's Use Of Examples In The *Topics*', p. 216, calls it 'a good example of sophistical argumentation'.
[119] 'Dialectic And Eristic In The Treatment Of The Forms', pp. 118–19.
[120] Aristotle indicates at 146b37 – 'and in all the other cases where it applies' – that the usefulness of the topic is not restricted to problems about appetites.
[121] cf. pp. 60–1 above.

of wish gave rise to the paradoxical consequence that the man who wishes wrongly did not wish at all; and it was in order to avoid this paradox and to preserve what was valuable in the realist position that Aristotle introduced his distinction between the unqualified and the qualified object of wish, a distinction which lessened the gulf between appearance and reality. In *Top.* Z8 we see the extreme realist clearly identified with the adherent of the theory of Forms; and we learn how adherence to this theory must lead him to the assertion of paradox. The argument in *Top.* Z8 shows that the Platonist cannot *both* maintain the theory of Forms *and* allow that the definition should mention what *appears*. *EN* Γ4 and *Top.* Z8 present what is essentially the same objection against the same theory, although the *Ethics* emphasises the difficulties which this theory affords to the notion of wish and the *Topics* emphasises the difficulties for the notion of the object of wish. But for the historian the *Topics* contributes the valuable information that the authors of the theory included the Platonists.

The argument in *Top.* Z8 is markedly similar to the final argument against the Forms in Plato's *Parmenides*.[122] That argument also turns on the relation between faculties and their objects, and it too employs a thesis about the logic of correlatives. The interpretation of the force of the arguments in the *Parmenides* against the theory of Forms as it is presented in earlier dialogues, and of Plato's purpose in producing these arguments, has, of course, been a point of major controversy in Platonic scholarship during the past century. Critical reaction to the arguments as a whole has ranged from those who maintain that they have no damaging effect on the theory and that they trade on misinterpretations of the theory,[123] to those who find in at least some of the arguments clear indication that Plato was modifying or abandoning some of his earlier position. Probably the most common opinion now is that the arguments do exploit serious weaknesses in the earlier theory, although the full seriousness of the difficulties may not have been grasped by Plato himself;[124] and the tendency of my analysis of one of the arguments will be in support of this opinion. But most of the discussion has touched on this particular argument only slightly. It has concentrated on the regress arguments,[125] despite the fact that Plato signals the argument about knowledge as a very great difficulty[126] and clearly an attack on the status of the Forms as objects of knowledge subverts Plato's

---

[122] 133b–134e.

[123] For example, Cherniss, 'The Relation of the *Timaeus* to Plato's Later Dialogues'; Peck, 'Plato's *Parmenides*: some suggestions for its interpretation'.

[124] G. E. L. Owen, 'A Proof in the *Peri Ideōn*', p. 105; C. Strang, 'Plato and the Third Man'.

[125] 132a–133a. [126] 133b.

metaphysical theory even more fundamentally than the other attacks on aspects of their nature.

The argument moves from the premises that Forms are objects of knowledge and are distinct from the things which participate in them, to the conclusion that they are not objects of *our* knowledge. It makes crucial use of the *endoxon* which is also used in *Top.* Z8 – that Forms are correlative with each other and that a Form is not correlative with something other than a Form. A consequence of this *endoxon* is that the many instances which participate in the Form, being distinct from it, are not correlative with the Form but must rather be correlative with each other.[127] The thesis is illustrated with the case of Master and Slave: here each Form will be correlative with the other and with nothing else, and each particular master with a particular slave and vice versa. If we apply the thesis to knowledge and its objects, then Knowledge (the Form) is of Reality (the Forms); and this holds both of Knowledge in general, which has Reality in general as its object, and of the special sciences, each of which has a part of Reality as its object.[128] On the other hand, *someone's* knowledge – in general, *our* knowledge – is something which participates in the Form of Knowledge (or in one of the Forms of the special sciences). Such knowledge, therefore, cannot be of the Forms: it must be of the instances which participate in and are distinct from the Forms. The latter alone are objects of Knowledge, but not of *our* knowledge.[129] Moreover the distinction between Forms and particulars is not simply one between the general and the specific. The Knowledge that is the Form exceeds in precision the instances of knowledge that participate in it, as with every Form and its instances. It follows, by the *endoxon* once again, that whereas the objects of precise Knowledge (the Form) are the most precise things (the Forms), both our knowledge and its objects are imprecise things.[130]

This conclusion conflicts, of course, with cherished Platonic theories about the power of the human soul, by dialectic and recollection, to become aware of the Forms. But just this makes this argument a serious difficulty for Plato, provided that its premises are his and the reasoning is valid. We may briefly consider two objections which have been raised against the reasoning.[131] Firstly, it has been claimed that the argument ignores the relation between a Form and the things which participate in it. On the contrary, the argument recognises this relation but insists that the things so related

---

[127] 133c–133d.   [128] 134a3–7.

[129] 134a9–134c2.   [130] 134c–134e.

[131] One or other of these objections appear in Cherniss, *Aristotle's Criticism of Plato and the Academy*, vol. i, p. 282; Runciman, 'Plato's *Parmenides*', p. 98; Vlastos, 'The Third Man Argument in the *Parmenides*', p. 346.

are distinct: it is concerned with a different relation, which I have called 'correlation' and which it declares not to hold between, for example, a particular master and the Form Slave. Secondly, insofar as the argument contrasts Knowledge and our knowledge in respect of their precision and that of the objects which each has, it has been regarded as just one more example of a difficulty which exploits a view of Forms as both *being* and *having* a given character (the 'self-predication assumption'). If this is so, our argument loses the special interest which I believe it to have. A full discussion of this point would take us too far afield. But it is not at all clear how the self-predication assumption is to be interpreted in the case of such a concept as *object of knowledge*. In fact it is plausible to say that such a thing is (predicatively) an object of knowledge. Moreover, if we wish to distinguish between general and paradigm forms of the concepts of knowledge and its objects, the argument can be divided into two parts – 134a–134b and 134c–134d – each of which will promote the undesired conclusion that such objects cannot be objects of the knowledge *of one of us*.

The theory of Forms

The crux of the matter lies in the *endoxon* about correlatives. What we have in the *Parmenides* argument is an application of a general logical principle which is advanced by Plato in the *Republic*.[132] The principle is endorsed in a context where the distinction between Forms and particulars is not at all in view. The context also contains Plato's statement of the principle of non-contradiction,[133] which is likewise free from commitment to any ontology. But, as I shall maintain, both this and the principle of correlatives are powerful influences in the devising of the theory of Forms; and for this reason it is particularly damaging when the *Parmenides* shows how the principle of correlatives can be turned against the theory.

The logical principle states that two correlative things must each be similarly qualified or unqualified. Thus thirst *simply* is a desire for drink *simply*; but if we qualify the thirst and consider, for example, a *great* thirst, the drink to which the thirst is related must also be qualified as a *great amount* of drink.[134] In this passage we also find the example of knowledge and its correlate – a study;[135] as with thirst and drink, knowledge and study must both be qualified or unqualified.[136]

[132] IV, 438.   [133] IV, 436.   [134] 437e.

[135] Thus I translate '*mathēma*'. Plato is uncertain here how to characterise the object of knowledge (438c7–8). In its characterisation of this object the *Parmenides* makes perfectly fair use of the epistemological component of the theory of Forms.

[136] 438c6–438d9.

Two features of the language used in this passage should be noted. The first concerns the use of '*autos*' – best translated here as 'in itself' or 'as such' – to designate the unqualified form of each concept under discussion. Now although, as I have said, the distinction between Forms and particulars is not in view here, it is noteworthy that the use of '*autos*' with a general term is one of Plato's devices for marking off a Form from its related particulars. The most likely explanation of this use is that it functions in the same way as such modern typographical devices as underlinings: by coupling '*autos*' with a word Plato wishes to concentrate our attention on what is signified by that word alone.[137] The theory of Forms uses this device to show that each Form is simple in nature, an object whose nature is exhaustively indicated by the particular name used: particulars, by contrast, are many other things in addition to what is signified by any general term by which they may be called.[138] The function of '*autos*' in the context of this theory, then, is to mark an abstraction which occurs in the nature of things. While this aim is not a feature of the argument about correlatives in *Republic* IV, this discussion too is concerned to mark off, as an abstraction, the unqualified form of a concept from the qualified forms.

The second striking feature of the language is the use of '*haplōs*' – 'without qualification' – to mark the distinction between the general and the specific forms of such a concept as knowledge. At 438e6–8 Plato says that if we specify certain objects of knowledge as *medical*, this causes 'it no longer to be called without qualification knowledge but, with the addition of the particular qualification, medical knowledge'. We have examined the crucial use which Aristotle makes of the distinction between the qualified and the unqualified in his analysis of the relation between faculties and their objects. That analysis seeks to correct what Aristotle perceives to be a defect in Plato's metaphysics; and the first indication that the defect is built into the theory of Forms comes in the argument in the *Parmenides*. This argument, in turn, relies on a principle which the *Republic* presents in language which will figure prominently in later stages of the debate. These two linguistic features make it the more likely that the later arguments will expose serious difficulties in the theory of Forms. But to confirm this, we must briefly review the theory itself.

If we survey the comparatively few passages in which Plato comments on the distinctions between Forms and particulars, the

---

[137] I follow G. E. L. Owen, 'Dialectic and Eristic in the Treatment of the Forms', p. 115.

[138] Some texts which suggest this clearly are *Crat.* 439d3–5; *Phaedo* 100c; *Rep.* 476a.

single most emphasised point is that contrary Forms are quite distinct from one another. Phenomenal particulars are marked by the copresence of contraries, but with Forms this is not so.[139] Plato makes this point a number of times by saying that the Form X, unlike the particulars of type X, cannot take as predicate the character corresponding to the Form which is contrary to X.[140] This leaves it unclear whether the relation between the word 'X' and the Form is that of a name or a description, although it may be taken to lend some force to the former interpretation. But this is an issue which we can leave undecided as, I maintain, it is left open in the *Parmenides* argument.

The function of Forms is to resolve difficulties in our understanding of things.[141] Plato takes the stance of the realist and seeks to maintain, against relativists and sceptics who would query it, that the ground for distinguishing expert from inexpert judgement is the degree to which each has insight into the objective nature of things. The terms in which the debate is conducted revolve around the ability to discriminate between contraries. Because the relativists maintained that there could be no such ability,[142] Plato's reply is to explore the epistemic conditions for grasping the real basis of the distinction between contraries.

Not only in general terms but also in detail Plato's Forms are designed to counter the relativist's theses. The latter exploited the qualifications that can attach to contrary things in respect of variations over time, differences of part or aspect, relations with other things, and the various persons involved. Thus the same thing can be shown to be both good and bad – and likewise for other contrary predicates – if these predicates are indexed by reference to these types of factor. It should be noted that one factor which is *absent* from such indexing is a reference to the different *views* that different persons may take of the same thing. If this were present, it would beg the question in favour of relativism: as it is, reference to the types of factors which *are* mentioned is intended to support an argument from which relativism can be *deduced*.

Plato's response is to acknowledge that the relativist's examples correctly report the facts with which he is familiar, but to maintain that these are not all the facts relevant to the case and therefore to challenge the relativist's conclusion. Access to the Forms supplies us with the necessary extra facts. As a direct counter to the relativist's

[139] *Phaedo* 74b–74c, 102c–103c; *Symp.* 211a; *Rep.* 476a, 479a–479c, 525d–526a; *Parm.* 129.
[140] For example, *Phaedo* 103b, *Parm.* 129b.
[141] This has been realised by philosophers from Aristotle, *Met.* M4, 1078b12–17, to J. L. Austin, 'Are There *A Priori* Concepts?', pp. 2–5.
[142] A valuable text is *Dissoi Logoi* 1–3 (Diels-Kranz, *Die Fragmente der Vorsokratiker*, vol. 2, pp. 405–11); see G. Ryle, *Plato's Progress*, p. 214.

exploitation of the qualifications that can attach to contraries in a context, Forms are specified as free from temporal variation, simple in nature, not relative to different things,[143] and not relative to different persons. Once more, it is to be noted that the last heading is better *not* interpreted as denying that the same Form may be *viewed* differently by different persons. No text requires to be interpreted thus;[144] and it would have the effect of begging the case in favour of realism.

This contrast between Forms and particulars can best be represented as a distinction between context-free and context-dependent cases of concepts. For example, we distinguish the claim that something is good (simply) or one (simply) from the claim that it is a good *F* (e.g. man, thief) or one *F* (page, book). In this idiom context-free uses of words, when these are properly construed, designate only Forms, while the references of the context-dependent uses will be particulars. Now the principle of non-contradiction as stated in *Republic* IV makes allowance for the qualifications which need to be added in the case of context-dependent uses of contrary words. To this extent Plato shows that the relativist's examples are compatible with metaphysical realism: a statement which uses a context-dependent word is still true or false.[145] But evidently he feels that this is so only because the context-dependent uses of words derive their meanings from the context-free uses, and that it can be grasped to be so only by one who is aware of those things – the Forms – which by their nature are not liable to the variations imposed by context.

This is the basis of his argument that it is of the nature of Forms to be objects of knowledge and of the nature of particulars to be objects of belief.[146] Instead of realising that it is possible to distinguish an expert from an inexpert view of things whether those things are context-free or context-dependent, Plato assigns the former things to be the objects of the expert's understanding and the latter to be objects of inexpert (mis)understanding. *Now* we can attach to particulars the type of qualification that mentions the

[143] Since some Forms, e.g. Master and Knowledge, evidently are relative, there is a problem which we cannot explore here. See Aristotle, *Peri Ideōn*, fr. 5 (Ross) and the discussion by G. E. L. Owen, 'A Proof in the *Peri Ideōn*'. But even so such Forms are invariant (tenselessly) in their relations.

[144] Many commentators, most recently D. Gallop, *Plato Phaedo*, pp. 122–3, fail to perceive how radically this interpretation of such texts as *Phaedo* 74b differs from the available alternatives.

[145] C. Kirwan, 'Plato and relativity', pp. 119–20, is to be commended for bringing *Rep.* IV into the discussion of the theory of Forms but, in my view, underestimates its importance.

[146] *Rep.* V, 479.

person in whose view something has a certain character. For Plato's argument has sought to show, as a conclusion and not as a premiss, that realism depends on the existence of the Forms and that those who are unaware of them are committed to metaphysical relativism.

In this way the qualifications and lack of them which attach respectively to particulars and Forms are given a metaphysical interpretation. The objects of a person's inexpert belief are now qualified as objects of *his* belief: they are the world as it seems to him. By contrast, the Forms are not subject to qualifications. So they are not such as to *seem* to anyone. Once the interpretation of being qualified and unqualified is extended in this way, we can show how the principle of correlatives, as presented in *Republic* IV, operates upon the situation. As sets of beliefs vary from person to person so does the world as it seems to each. Here, then, a subject's understanding is qualified to the extent to which the object of his understanding is qualified. But expert understanding, or knowledge, is not something that varies from person to person. Such understanding is not qualified by reference to its human subject: no more, in Plato's theory, are its objects – the Forms – subject to qualification.

Thus we see how Plato's search for the foundations of realist metaphysics moves by stages to a position which applies the principle of correlatives to knowledge and its objects. While this principle is first presented without reference to the theory of Forms, it nonetheless employs tools of analysis that are used in drawing the distinction between Forms and particulars. This is what makes its application in the *Parmenides*, as well as in *Top*. Z8, both effective and justified. For these arguments point up the consequences of applying the principle to the relation between human faculties and their objects. They show that insofar as each person's faculty is subject to the qualification of being *his*, its object cannot be *the* object of the faculty: moreover, if some exercise of the faculty may be counted an unqualified exercise in virtue of its expertness, its object cannot be something other than the object of the faculty. In terms of the distinction between Forms and particulars, this makes it incoherent to assert, as Plato does in the *Republic*,[147] that the expert recognises the distinctness of the two, while the inexpert confuse them.

We have explored in detail Aristotle's analysis of the relation between faculties and their objects, and have shown how he is able to assert, against Plato, that what *appears* to the good man *is* so. His procedure is to reconsider Plato's principle of correlatives. He works with the contrasts between the unqualified and the qualified, the general and the particular, the simple and the complex. All this goes back to the discussion in *Republic* IV. But Aristotle revises the

---

[147] v, 476c4–476d3.

application of these contrasts across the correlations, so that he can say that the object of wish is at the same time the object of the good man's wish.[148] My purpose in the preceding pages has been to examine the continuity of these discussions, from the considerations which animate the theory of Forms, through the exposition and criticism of that theory by Plato, to Aristotle's examination and reformulation of the realist position.

The immense importance and originality of Plato's work in this area has been justly recognised. Aristotle's equally important contribution has tended to be overlooked. This is unfortunate, since Aristotle has the additional merit of being correct. What is also crucial to grasp is the large set of consequences, as to the nature of intellectual investigation and in particular of dialectic, that follow from the Aristotelian metaphysical analysis. Then we shall see how very much his own is his concept of dialectic.

[148] See pp. 60–1 above.

4

DEFINITION

Hitherto we have been considering the theoretical basis of Aristotle's dialectic. On the basis of comments in the *Topics* and in other works we have determined the function and scope of dialectic in relation to other types of enterprise. We also saw that the *Topics* declares itself to be a work which will proceed conformably with this notion of dialectic's nature.[1] In pursuing these ideas we have noticed a number of detailed ways in which the treatment in the *Topics* corroborates the general statements about dialectic. For example, it reflects the interest in the common predicates which are said in the *Metaphysics* to fall within the scope of dialectic; and it agrees with that work in recognising both the connection and the difference between dialectic and universal ontology with respect to the discovery of the foundations of knowledge.[2] A number of the key notions in dialectic, such as those of being more intelligible or endoxic, are analysed in the *Topics* according to the general theory which lies behind the work.[3]

This is still a theoretical characterisation of dialectic and of the *Topics*. I maintain that as such it has an importance and an interest independently of the extent to which it is reflected in practice in the detailed discussions in the *Topics*. But it is clearly valuable to consider this latter issue; and, for the sake of illustration, I propose to examine certain features of Aristotle's treatment of definition in the *Topics*. According to the theory of statements in this work, each statement expresses one of four possible relations between the things for which its subject and predicate terms stand.[4] One of these relations is that of being a definition; and the treatment of such statements occupies *Top.* Z–H, which is slightly less than a quarter of the whole work and represents a considerably larger space than the discussion of any of the other three types of statement.[5]

We shall be examining three issues in the material that occupies

---

[1] See pp. 89–94 above.　　　　[2] Chapter two above.
[3] pp. 68–85 above.　　　　[4] *Top.* A4, 101b17–36.
[5] It has been examined by W. A. de Pater, in *Les Topiques d' Aristote et la Dialectique Platonicienne*. In my view the greatest value of this, at times rather episodic work, lies in its analysis of the notion of a topic (chapter two).

Top. Z–H, which I have selected for two reasons. Firstly, they form part of important areas of problems in Aristotle's theory of definition and receive attention in other works besides the *Topics*: the discussions in the *Topics* make a useful contribution to the general interpretation of Aristotle's views on these matters. Secondly, the special character of the discussions in the *Topics* can be shown by such an examination to conform to the pattern of dialectical analysis which has been argued for in the earlier parts of this investigation. For we have seen that the nature of dialectic is determined by the fact that it employs certain concepts which, as Aristotle's analysis shows, possess a double type of universality; these are the type of universality which characterises the concept in its central and primary form, and the type which characterises it in all its forms, peripheral as well as central.[6] It was the distinction between these two forms of universality which was the basis for the analysis of the relation between dialectic and science. But we must also recognise that these concepts are unitary, despite their complexity, and that to fragment them is to make the mistake of those whose analyses of them Aristotle opposes in *EN* Γ4. Consequently, we might expect that in the detailed treatment in the *Topics* Aristotle's concern is not exclusively *either* with the concepts in their absolute form *or* with them in their qualified forms, but rather with the connection between these two forms. I believe that this emerges clearly in the discussion of problems of definition in *Top.* Z–H which we are about to examine. Aristotle conducts these discussions against the background of current practice; but at the same time he is conscious of an ideal of definition, and uses insights derived from it, which was not fully available to those whose practice is reflected in the discussions. But this ideal works unobtrusively in the *Topics*. The effect of the discussions is to reinforce it obliquely, by showing the consequences of ignoring it in terms which would be readily intelligible to those who do not fully appreciate it.

Genus, differentia and essence

In *Top.* A5 a definition is defined as 'a set of words (*logos*) which indicates the essence (*ti ēn einai*)'.[7] In the previous chapter[8] Aristotle had asserted that definitions indicate the essence: he thereby distinguishes them from properties which are like definitions in indicating characteristics possessed exclusively by the subject. The claim that definitions indicate the essence of the subject is not further justified or discussed in *Top.* A. But in A5 there is some discussion, although no justification, of the claim that the definition

---

[6] See pp. 64–7 above   [7] 101b38.   [8] A4, 101b19–23.

must be of more than one word. Aristotle allows that single word identifications, of such forms as 'X is Y' or 'X is the same as Y', are 'definitory'; but he will not allow that they are definitions.[9] The reason for this concession is that the tactics which are useful in dealing with expressions of this form will also, but to a limited extent, be useful in dealing with definitions; the extent is limited, because whereas refutation of the claim that X is the same as Y constitutes refutation of the claim that Y is the definition of X, establishing that X is the same as Y is not equivalent to establishing that Y is the definition of X.[10] In *Top.* A7 Aristotle states that identity in its most readily agreed form, i.e. numerical identity, may hold between a subject and its property or between a subject and its accident,[11] or in a more fundamental way it may hold between what is designated by two names or by a name and an expression the meanings of which, in each case, are the same.[12] The identity, then, which holds between what is designated by the name and the defining expression is only one of the forms which numerical identity may take. So when Aristotle says in *Top.* A5 that the manoeuvres appropriate for dealing with claims of the form 'X is the same as Y' only partially coincide with those appropriate for dealing with definitions, his remarks are consistent with the analysis of the forms of identity which he offers in *Top.* A7.

These two basic assumptions about the character of definitions in the statement of *Top.* A – that they must be expressions of more than one word, and that they must indicate the essence – are reflected in the discussion of *Top.* Z–H, where once again they are unquestioned assumptions. That the definition must be a *logos* and not a single word is assumed in the statement of the first condition for adequate definitions in the introduction to the book;[13] and it is indicative of the basic nature of this assumption that we do not find a topic which attacks proposed definitions for consisting only of single words.[14] The same uncompromising attitude can be seen in the strictures of *Top.* Z11, 148b33–149a7, on definitions which have the same number of words as the expressions designating the subject of the definition. Such definitions take the form 'XYZ is the

---

[9] 102a2–17.

[10] 102a11–17; cf. *Top.* H2, 152b36–153a5.

[11] 103a27–31. [12] 103a23–7.

[13] The *logos* must be true of that of which the name is true, Z1, 139a25–7.

[14] Some examples of single word definitions occur at Z2, 139b33–4, 140a4–5: 'The Earth is a Nurse', 'The Eye is Brow-Shaded'. These definitions are here attacked for their obscurity. It is not in fact clear that the examples given here are intended to be complete definitions; but even if they are, the very obvious degree of poetic licence which characterises them makes it unlikely that they had a serious place in the intellectual environment from which Aristotle's reflections on definition arose.

definition of *ABC'*, so that there is a one–one correspondence between the linguistic elements in the subject and in the definition. Aristotle rejects such definitions on the very ground that they simply substitute a single word for each word in the expression which designates the subject, instead of substituting an expression for the single word.[15] In works other than the *Topics* Aristotle frequently expresses the requirement that the definition must be an expression which contains more than one word.

Similarly, the requirement that the definition indicate the essence (*ti ēn einai*) is an unargued premiss to the discussion in *Top.* Z–H.[16] Elsewhere in Aristotle's works the axiomatic character of this requirement can be seen. Thus, at *Met.* Z4, 1030a6–7, he says that a thing has an essence only if the expression which describes its nature is a definition. This statement follows an analysis which has rejected the claim of certain things (compounds of items from more than one category) to have essences, on the grounds of linguistic considerations concerning the descriptions of their natures. The 'names' of such compounds do not, strictly, *name* anything as such but rather assert one thing of another; and 1030a6–7 is a recapitulation rather than a fresh deduction from the preceding argument. As a statement it is of great importance to the understanding of the strategy adopted by Aristotle in his investigation of the principles of beings in *Met.* Z–H; for the premiss that the nature of definition is a mirror in language of the nature of essence lies behind the detailed attention which Aristotle devotes to questions of definition in Z4–6, 10–12, 15, 17, and H2–3. Similarly there are many places in the *Analytics* where he connects the notions of definition and essence.[17] In the body of the discussion of definition in *Top.* Z–H the expression '*ti ēn einai*' appears a number of times: Z4, 141b24–5; Z5, 143a17–19, Z8, 146b32; H3, 153a14–22; 154a32. These passages contain ideas which will be considered in the following pages. Their effect is to connect the notion of essence with such related notions as that of genus and differentia. The discussion at *Top.* H3 is particularly important, since here the assertion that the definition is a 'set of words which shows the thing's essence' forms the first step in the controversial argument that it is possible to establish a definition.[18] But in themselves these passages leave unresolved the question

---

[15] 149a1–4: 'No more names have been uttered now than before, whereas the definer should replace names by phrases'.

[16] Z1, 139a32–4: 'He has not defined and has not expressed the essence of the thing being defined'; Z4, 141a24–5: 'Consider whether he has defined and has expressed the essence or not.'

[17] e.g. *An. Post.* A22, 82b37–9; B6, 92a7, 9; B8, 93a19.

[18] The controversy is too large a question to enter into here. Different commentators have argued that the argument in *Top.* H3 shows the *Topics* to be an earlier work than the *Posterior Analytics* (e.g. Maier, *Die Syllogistik*

of what Aristotle supposed to be the relation between his conception of essence and the more familiar notion of definition.

A further idea which we must rank among the assumptions which underlie the treatment of definition in the *Topics* is (1) that the predicates which make up the *logos* of the subject should answer the question 'what is it?'[19] and (2) that these predicates can be classified into two types – genus and differentia. The status of these assumptions, however, is more problematic than that of those discussed above; there are difficulties both about each of them and about their combination. In this complex of ideas the element which appears most frequently and which we can assert with most confidence to be basic to the discussion of definition is that which regards the genus as predicated 'as part of the nature'. For this there is ample evidence. Thus at A5, 102a31–2, the genus is defined as 'that which is predicated of a number of specifically differing things as part of their nature'.[20] This idea is also integral to the account of the doctrine of categories in *Top*. A9. When we are presented with any item, whatever its category, to give the name either of the subject or of its genus is to indicate its nature.[21] As to the differentia, while at *Top*. A4, 101b18–19, questions relating to it are said to fall under the same head as those relating to the genus, and at H3, 153a17–18, and H5, 154a27–8, no difficulty is expressed about speaking of differentiae as 'predicated as part of the nature', nevertheless at Δ6, 128a20–9, it is said to be the view only of some that the differentia is predicated of the species as part of its nature. In this passage of Δ6 Aristotle recommends that those who maintain

des Aristoteles, vol. II.2, p. 78 n. 3) or a work of essentially less serious intent than the *Posterior Analytics* (e.g. Cherniss, *Aristotle's Criticism of Plato and the Academy*, p. 34 n. 28). Both arguments rely on the fact that in *An. Post*. B6 an argument for the establishing of definitions which is apparently the same as that of *Top*. H3 is rejected as a *petitio principii*. The brief answer to this is that in *An. Post*. B6 Aristotle rejects a form of proof which contains as one of its premisses a definition of Definition, and compares such a form of proof with the proof which would attempt to establish a syllogism by presenting the definition of Syllogism as one of the premisses (92a11–19). But he is not arguing that it is impossible to establish a syllogism; and equally, the fact that *petitio principii* is possible on the part of those who attempt to establish definitions does not mean that all attempts to establish definitions are doomed to commit this fallacy. A comparison of *An. Post*. 92a7–9 with *Top*. 153a18–20 shows that the argument in *An. Post*. contains, as that in the *Topics* does not, a mention of the definition of Definition.

[19] *Top*. H3, 153a16–17: they are predicated of the subject 'as part of its nature (*ti esti*)'.

[20] cf. further *Top*. A18, 108b22–3; Δ1, 120b21–9; Δ6, 127b27–31; E3, 132a10–13; Z5, 142b23–9.

[21] 103b35–7. One of the results of the argument of this chapter is to exclude the claims of any item in a category other than that of the subject to be the genus of the subject.

this view of the differentia should be confronted with the following comments: it is more suitable to offer the genus than the differentia in reply to questions about the nature of the subject, and furthermore whereas the differentia always qualifies the genus, the converse is not the case. This comment recalls Δ2, 122b16–17, which says 'no differentia indicates a nature (*ti esti*) but rather some qualified thing (*poion ti*)' in justification of an objection against those who offer a differentia as a genus. In the same vein are the remarks at Z6, 144a18–19, 'the differentia is felt to indicate some qualified thing', and at 144a20–2, 'see whether the differentia indicates some individual thing rather some qualified thing; for every differentia is felt to show some qualified thing'.

But there are a number of passages that seem to tell in the opposite direction. At Z6, 145a3–12, Aristotle rejects the idea that an affection (*pathos*) can be a differentia, with the following comment: 'every affection, as it increases in degree, dislodges a thing from its being, whereas the differentia is not like this; for the differentia is felt rather to conserve that of which it is the differentia, and it is simply impossible for there to be each thing without its own differentia, – if it is not footed, it will not be a man'. Similarly at E4, 132b35–133a5, those who offer as a property of a subject what is in fact its differentia, are attacked on the grounds that the differentia 'contributes to the essence (*ti ēn einai*)', which the property must not do. But while these passages provide evidence for a connection between the concept of differentia and those of being (*ousia*) and essence they do not provide the link between the differentia and the nature (*ti esti*) with which I am now concerned. Indeed two passages in *Top.* E which in conjunction tell in favour of a link between differentia and essence tell *against* a link between the differentia and the nature. The topic at E3, 132a10–21, requires that the property-expression should include an element which expresses the nature of the subject, and it says that this element should be the genus. But the topic at E3, 131b37–132a9, requires that the property-expression should *not* 'show the essence', since then it would be a definition. So of the two elements in the definition – genus and differentia – it must be the differentia which is inadmissible in the property-expression and, therefore, not part of the nature.

To turn now to the connection between genus/differentia and definition (rather than between genus/differentia and essence or nature), the evidence is implicit rather than explicit, and such explicit evidence as exists is of a rather equivocal nature. *Top.* Z1 urges us to examine whether the definition contains mention of the subject's proper genus, on the following grounds: 'he who defines must place the thing in a genus and add the differentiae; for of the things in the definition the genus is felt most to indicate the being of the thing defined' (139a28–31). Here the words 'is felt' qualify the injunction; since it is fundamental to Aristotle's theory that the definition should express the essence of the subject, the qualification must relate to doubts about the suitability of the genus to do this and thus about its suitability for a place in the definition.[22] A comment in Z4 is similarly qualified: '*given that* he who defines properly must define by genus and differentiae and these are among the things that are without qualification more intelligible than and prior to the species' (141b25–8). This comment is advanced in support of the proposition that definitions which employ concepts which are more intelligible and prior *to us* can express the essence of the subject only if the concepts are also more intelligible and prior *absolutely*.[23] It is tempting to interpret it as simply *asserting* that a proper definition should employ those concepts – that is, the appropriate genus and differentia – which are prior and more intelligible. But this interpretation telescopes Aristotle's argument. Rather, Aristotle says that (1) he who defines 'properly (*kalōs*)' should give the genus and differentia, and (2) these are prior and more intelligible. (2) needs to be proved, and this is done at 141b28–34. When (2) has been established, it certainly follows that definition *must* be by genus and differentia. But (1) stands in the text as a premiss to the argument, and it is a mistake to read it as having the same meaning as the conclusion. The clue to the force of (1) lies in the word 'properly': this word indicates that we have to do here with considerations of the *manner of presenting* the definition rather than of the *substance* of the definition. Both *Top*. E and Z contain topics 'for doing it properly';[24] and it is clear from E2, 129b24–9, and E4, 132a22–6, that these topics are unable positively to establish that a given property or definition is true of the subject, and can only establish that it passes *one* of the tests which might have disqualified its claim.[25] In effect, then, what Aristotle says at Z4, 141b25–7, is that a definition composed of genus and differentia is well formed. But the considerations which relate to the correct form of the definition are not the same as those which relate to whether the definition has expressed the essence of the subject.[26] So this text

[22] Note also similar qualifications at 139a27; cf. Z5, 142b22.
[23] The general metaphysical significance of the ideas in this passage has been discussed on pp. 68–74 above.
[24] E2–3, Z2–3.
[25] In Book E the typical formula at the conclusion of these topics is: 'the property would hold properly *in this respect*'. Although the topics that establish in an unqualified way that the property or definition holds also establish that it holds properly, they are distinguished from the topics for doing it properly (132a24–6).
[26] cf. the distinction at *Top*. Z4, 141a23–5.

does not enable one to say with confidence that it is a basic premiss to Aristotle's view of definition in the *Topics* that the definition should be composed of genus and differentia. It suggests rather that Aristotle felt it necessary to prove the point. Undeniably the genus/differentia model of definition plays an extremely important part in *Top.* Z–H. Aristotle uses it in Z4 to show the detailed application of his thesis that the elements of the definition must be prior and more intelligible absolutely than the subject. Z5 is devoted to consideration of the genus, as is Z6 to the differentia; and in H3 and 5 this model of definition plays a crucial part in the argument that it is possible to establish the definition.[27] But it is also true that some of the topics do not follow this model;[28] and the frequent use of the model is probably to be explained in terms of the intellectual background against which Aristotle's comments on the strategy for treating definitions are set, rather than as a consequence of the use to which he puts the model in the arguments of *Top.* Z4 and H3.[29] That there was indeed such a background is clear from such remarks as those at *PA* A2, 642b5–6, '*some people* grasp the particular by dividing the *genus* into two *differentiae*' and at *Met.* H6, 1045a20–2, 'it is clear that those who proceed to define and speak *in this customary way* cannot explain and resolve the difficulty', which refers back to the discussion in *Met.* Z12 of definitions by genus and differentia.[30] These ideas appear in a number of texts in Plato. At *Philebus* 12e there is a contrast between the unity of the genus and the contrariety and difference (*diaphorotēs*) which is found in its parts; and at *Sophist* 253d he speaks of the dialectician's ability to see 'many forms, different from one another, contained by one form external to them'. But the text which most clearly shows these ideas is *Politicus* 285a7–285b6:

The right course is firstly, whenever one at first sees that many things are linked, not to turn away until one detects in this all the *differentiae* which reside in *species*, and secondly, whenever various dissimilarities are seen in masses of things, not to be capable of being put off and stopping until one has secured within a single similarity all that belongs there and surrounded it with the being of some *genus*.

The details of the recommendations in this passage are very debatable; but it is at least clear that they make use of the trio genus/

---

27 It is further used at Z7, 146a33–5; Z8, 146b20–35; Z11, 149a14–28; Z12, 149a29–37.
28 The topics of Z13, which will be examined on pp. 114–17 below.
29 For further indication of a background of inherited practices, see the comment on differentiae at *Top.* A18, 108b4–6, '*we customarily* use the differentiae peculiar to each thing to mark off the special definition of each thing's being'.   30 cf. 1037b27–30.

differentia/species. Speusippus too, if we accept the commentators'
identification of the target of Aristotle's attack at *An. Post.* B13,
97a6–22, closely linked the notions of definition and difference.[31]

Nevertheless, these passages do not indicate that the various
notions which occur in them – essence, genus, differentia – had
been brought into a systematic relationship. Indeed the very
obscurity of the passages in the later dialogues where Plato discusses
method, suggests that he had no very clear idea of the model which
he is trying to describe; and the discrepancies in Aristotle's various
comments on the differentia in the *Topics* point in the same direction. It is now time to draw the strands together and consider what
the *Topics* reveals about Aristotle's own contribution to the clarifica-
tion of these notions about definition.

The definition must be an expression of more than one word and
must indicate the essence. The genus is predicated as part of the
nature of the subject, and the differentia indicates the essence. On
the other hand, it is less certain that the definition should contain
genus and differentia, or that being predicated as part of the nature
and indicating the essence are equivalent notions. The two expressions '*ti esti*' and '*ti ēn einai*' are frequently used interchangeably
to mean 'essential nature'.[32] But the first of these two expressions is
one which Aristotle has inherited from previous thinkers,[33] whereas
the second is in all probability his own coinage.[34] Much controversy
surrounds the meaning and purpose of the Aristotelian expression.
I should conjecture that his purpose in substituting the novel formula
for the conventional '*ti esti*' is to avoid paradoxes of the third-man
type which arise when universals are hypostasised: 'a man moves'
may carry the suggestion that universals are subject to change,
whereas 'for there to be a man is for it to move' does not.[35] But my
concern is not so much to interpret the expressions '*ti esti*' and '*ti ēn
einai*' as to emphasise the novelty of the latter in contrast to the
former.

The background from which Aristotle takes the former expression
also appears to provide the idea that the genus is the main indicator
of the nature of the definiendum. We should note that he uses

---

[31] cf. fr. 31a–31e (Lang).
[32] cf., e.g., *Met.* Z4 and Z5 where the same considerations are adduced to
show that '*ti esti*' (1030a17–18) and '*ti ēn einai*' (1031a7–11) are expressions of complex meaning: they attach primarily to substances and only
derivatively to things in other categories; *An. Post.* B6, 92a6–10.
[33] For Plato, cf. *Rep.* 524c11, *Theaet.* 146c4.
[34] cf. P. T. Geach and G. E. M. Anscombe, *Three Philosophers*, pp. 24–6.
Alexander (*In Topica* 42.20–2) and Diogenes Laertius (vi.3) attribute the
expression '*ti ēn*' to Antisthenes; but Alexander indicates that the addition
of '*einai*' is Aristotle's.
[35] cf. the arguments against the Forms at *Top.* 137b3–8, 148a14–22.

'partake' (*metechein*) to describe the relation of species to genus but not that of species to differentia.[36] This is the technical term used in the theory of Forms to describe the relation between something and the real element in things of that kind. Moreover in the Academy the word '*eidos*' connoted not only 'species' in the theory of division but also 'reality' in the ontological theory. Since '*genos*' shared with '*eidos*' the sense of 'kind', it would be natural that when the question of the real element in the species came to be considered, the notion of reality which attached to '*eidos*' should be extended to '*genos*'. This would explain why the genus, but not the differentia, was predicated as part of the subject's nature. This same background also provides the idea that definition should be by genus and differentia. But it seems that Aristotle did not find in previous theories of definition any attempt to relate the two elements in the picture – the notion that the genus indicates the nature of the subject, and the idea that the definition should be composed of genus and differentia. This failure to relate the two elements reflects a failure to reconcile two impulses which lie behind the search for definitions. The desire to discover the nature of the definiendum will produce something like the theory of division, which attempts to reveal the ways in which the subject is connected with and also distinguished from other subjects. On the other hand, the desire to discover the *real* nature of the subject brings into play questions of ontology; and these may not be easily accommodated to the model of definition which commends itself from the purely heuristic point of view.

I believe that this is the situation which confronted Aristotle when he considered the nature of definition. His reaction was to forge his own conception of the essential nature, the novelty of which he signals with the outlandish formula '*ti ēn einai*', and to link this conception firmly with the notion of the differentia which had occupied an uneasy position in the accounts of his predecessors. This becomes particularly clear in the argument of *Top.* Z4, 141a26–142a16, which combines a strongly realist view of definition with a concern for the genus/differentia model. In this argument Aristotle starts from the premiss that the definition must express the essence of the subject and that this essence is single,[37] and argues that there can only be one definition of each subject. A further premiss to the argument is that the elements of the definition must be prior to and more intelligible than the definiendum, since the purpose of definition is to increase the understanding;[38] and by an argument which we have already examined, he deduces that the

[36] *Top.* Δ1, 121a12, 30.
[37] 141a35; for this, cf. also *Top.* Z10, 148b14–16.
[38] 141a27–30.

elements of *the* definition must be prior and more intelligible absolutely. He then argues that the genus and differentia are prior and more intelligible absolutely than the subject;[39] and from this he concludes that *the* definition of the subject – i.e. the real and unique definition – must contain its genus and differentia. The effect of this argument, which is essentially Aristotelian in character, is to cement the links, which others had indicated but not fully developed, between the genus/differentia model of definition on the one hand and, on the other, the requirement that the definition should express the essence of the subject. For Aristotle *argues* that only if the definition contains the genus and the differentia, can it indicate the essence of the subject.

It is worth pausing for a moment to consider Aristotle's handling of these questions in the *Topics*, in the light of the general theory of dialectic which we examined earlier. We saw that because dialectic, unlike the sciences, is able to handle what is intelligible not only absolutely but also with reference to particular persons, it alone can make the connection between the concepts of these two kinds. Its concerns are limited neither to the absolute truth of the matter under consideration nor to the views held by persons on the matter: it embraces both of these and thus has the unique function of taking us from the latter to the former. Aristotle's comments in the *Topics* on definitions by genus and differentia conform with this pattern. For his procedure is to combine, over the various topics, considerations derived from what I have called 'the background' with considerations which are original to his own analysis. The resulting theoretical prescriptions for dialectical practice are very much in the character of the exercise as Aristotle conceives it to be.

The uniqueness of the definition: lists, parts and wholes

Despite the space and care which Aristotle devotes in the *Topics* to developing the theory of definition by genus and differentia, this model of definition does not entirely dominate the treatment in *Top.* Z. Chapter Z13 is given over to the examination of other kinds of definition, and it opens as follows: 'Consider also whether in giving a definition of something he has defined these things or what is from these things or this thing with this thing'. The latter part of this sentence alludes in general terms to the formulae in which such definitions are expressed; but we should not follow those translators who render these allusions in the formal mode and thereby make Aristotle concerned exclusively with the words of the definition, rather than with the things which such definitions present. For in this chapter, and in the associated contexts which we shall

[39] 141b27–34.

examine, he has some substantive points to make about things; and considerations of language are invoked to this end.

Definitions of the first kind mentioned – *these things* – are of the form 'X is Y and Z'; and against them Aristotle develops topics which consider the following kinds of case. He notes the possibility of a situation in which one person has the characteristic Y (but not Z) and another person has the characteristic Z (but not Y) and thus the two collectively would possess the characteristic X which neither possesses individually. For example, if Justice is defined as Temperance And Courage, we may have a situation in which one man is temperate but not courageous, and another is courageous but not temperate; and so the two would between them be just, although neither as an individual possesses the attribute.[40] If the paradoxical nature of this situation may be mitigated by considering the case in which the joint wealth of two people exceeds the personal wealth of either, we can imagine the situation in which one person has the characteristic Y and the contrary characteristic to Z, while the other person has the characteristic Z and the contrary characteristic to Y. Here the paradox is stronger; for if we accept that from the definition 'X is Y and Z' follows the definition 'The Contrary of X is The Contrary of Y And The Contrary of Z', the two people would collectively possess *both* the characteristic X *and* the characteristic contrary to X.[41] As for the move from the definition of X to that of the contrary of X, Aristotle argues elsewhere that the definitions of contrary subjects should themselves be contrary.[42] It should not be supposed that this move is evidence that Aristotle was unaware that the negation of a conjunction is equivalent to the negation of at least one, but not necessarily both, of the conjuncts. For he is concerned here not with the contradictory but with the contrary of the conjunction; and it is the contradictory of the conjunction which is the counterpart of the negation in the modern truth-functional rule.[43]

Aristotle sums up his comments on the ways of attacking definitions given in the form *these things* by noting that such definitions provide a conjunction of the parts of the subject rather than an account of the whole, and thus can be attacked by means of those considerations which show the whole to be something more than merely the conjunction of the parts.[44] The purpose of the whole/

---

[40] 150a3–7.   [41] 150a9–14.

[42] *Top.* Z9, 147a31–3; H3, 153a26–9.

[43] This is precisely the distinction between the cases envisaged in 150a4–7 and in 150a9–14. For the general distinction between contrary and contradictory statements cf. *De Int.* 7.

[44] 150a15–21; the grammatical connection with the preceding remarks makes it clear that these lines provide not a *new* line of attack but rather a generalisation of those already introduced.

part distinction is to indicate the unity of what can also be regarded as to some extent plural and would be regarded as *simply* plural in the absence of appreciation of the whole. The two men who are conjoined in the examples of 150a3–15 *are* simply plural and thus are not parts of anything; and yet they must be treated as parts if they can collectively fall under the subject X which is defined as Y And Z.

Similarly, Aristotle's treatment of definitions of the form *what is from these things* proceeds entirely within the terms of the whole/part distinction. The only example of such a definition which is given in this section is that of Shamelessness as From Courage And False Belief;[45] and it is clear from this example that, despite the apparent similarity between the topics at 150b22–6 and at Z14, 151a20–6, definitions of this form do not mention the fact that the parts which are conjoined by 'and' are organised to form a whole, but only suggest this by the use of 'from'. Definitions in this form may be attacked if (1) the parts are such as to be incapable of constituting a unity,[46] (2) the primary location[47] of the parts does not coincide with that of the whole,[48] (3) the parts are co-extensive in duration with the whole,[49] (4) there are variations in value between the parts and the whole,[50] (5) the whole is synonymous with any of the parts.[51]

Of definitions in the form *this thing with this thing* Aristotle says, firstly, that such definitions are reducible to either of the two forms which have already been considered, and accordingly, should such a reduction be allowed by one's opponent, the topics which have already been discussed will be serviceable.[52] Alternatively, attention should be directed to whether the two elements which are conjoined in the definition (1) can occur in the same bearer,[53] (2) can occur in the same place,[54] (3) can occur at the same time,[55] (4) are related to the same end as each other,[56] (5) are related to the same end as the subject.[57] These various means of attacking definitions in

---

[45] 150b3.   [46] 150a23–5.

[47] i.e. the prime bearer of the characteristic, cf. *Top.* Δ5, 126a3–16; *Met.* Δ23, 1023a24–5.

[48] 150a26–33.   [49] 150a33–6.

[50] 150a36–150b18; difficulties are expressed about the validity of this particular rule, but my concern here is with the general character of the topics which may be used against this form of definition, rather than with the details of them.

[51] 150b19–21; cf. *Met.* Λ4, 1070b4–10, where the fact that no element is the same as that which is compounded from the elements is used to show that there cannot be universal elements; the identity which Aristotle is speaking of is identity of type, and so the principle to which he appeals in *Met.* Λ4 is the same as that appealed to in *Top.* Z13.

[52] 150b27–32.   [53] 150b35–6.   [54] 150b36.

[55] 150b36.   [56] 151a2–6.   [57] 151a6–13.

this form are derived from an analysis of the senses of 'with';[58] and after presenting the various topics which are based on this analysis, Aristotle observes that some definitions of the form *this thing with this thing* do not use 'with' in any of the senses which this analysis has revealed, but indicate a relation which would be properly expressed by 'through'.[59] Such definitions can be attacked on the grounds that they simply fail to express what they intend.[60]

In the *Topics* there is only an implicit contrast between definitions of the types which are investigated in Z13 and those which give the genus and differentia and occupy the major part of the discussion in Z–H. But in other works we find this same contrast made explicit and turned to important use in the theory of definition. At *Met.* B3, 998a21–998b14, Aristotle debates the two sides to the problem of B1, 995b27–9, 'whether the principles and elements are the genera or the constituents into which each thing is divided'. In 998a21–998b11 the contrast between the two sides in this debate is presented in terms of the contrast between the constituent parts into which a thing can be analysed and the universals by means of which a thing is defined. But at 998b11–14 there is a shift in the terms of the contrast, with a consequent hardening of the *aporia*. Aristotle appeals to the requirement that there can only be one formula which expresses the essence of each subject – a requirement which we have already seen him using in *Top.* Z4 in his proof that the definition must contain elements which are prior and more intelligible absolutely. From this he argues that we cannot allow the title of definition to both of the accounts – that which gives the constituent parts, and that which gives the generic universals –, and consequently that only one of these two types of thing can be principles (*archai*). In 998a21–998b11 the contrast was between the claims of the constituent parts and of the elements of the definition to be *principles*; but in 998b11–14 this becomes a contrast between two types of definition. A somewhat similar contrast is found at *De An.* A1, 403a25–403b19, where Aristotle distinguishes the two types of definition which may be given of such a thing as a House – 'a shelter which prevents destruction by wind, storm and heat' and 'stones, bricks and wood'. Here he presents the contrast in terms of the distinction between matter and form; but there is in fact a close connection between the problem as it is expressed in *De An.* A1 and in *Met.* B3. This is clear from the discussion of this problem in *Met.* Z10–11. In these chapters Aristotle works together into a single discussion of the problem of the elements of the definition,

---

[58] cf. 150b33.   [59] 151a14–19.

[60] cf. *Top.* B3, 110b8–15; Z2, 139b28–31, for the recommendation that where our opponent uses an ambiguous word, we should disprove his claim by showing that it holds in none of the senses of the word.

both consideration of the constituent parts of the definiendum and consideration of the relation between material and formal parts in the nature of the subject.[61]

These texts from works other than the *Topics* show that the opposition between two types of definition which is implicit in the *Topics* is explicit in other works and forms the starting point for the fundamental discussions of the theory of definition which are found in those works. They also show that the predominant attention devoted in the *Topics* to the genus/differentia model of definition is a reflection of the same attitude as appears in the assumption of *Met.* B3[62] that definition, as opposed to other ways of describing the nature of a thing, proceeds in terms of the universals under which the subject falls. In fact, the contrast between the two types of definition appears to go back at least to the *Theaetetus*, where there is a distinction between a *logos* which enumerates the parts of the subject and one which gives the mark by which the subject differs from all else.[63]

It should be noted that in *Top.* Z Aristotle refrains from using the argument that each subject can only have one definition, as a means of attacking definitions which are given in the forms discussed in *Top.* Z13. It seems clear that this line of attack was open to him. Now there is indeed a sense of 'part (*meros*)' in which the genus and differentia are parts of the species[64] and a sense of 'from (*ek*)' in which the species is compounded from the differentia (and also, presumably, the genus);[65] and thus it might be thought that the topics of Z13, which are mainly concerned with the whole/part relation, could be applied to genus/differentia definitions. Nevertheless Aristotle distinguishes the senses of the words 'part' and 'from something' in which they describe the relations between genus, differentia and species, from other senses in which these relations would not correctly be so described.[66] Since the examples considered in *Top.* Z13 involve things which are parts or compounds in some sense other than that in which the genus, differentia and species are, the uniqueness requirement for definitions would rule out the possibility of the co-existence of a definition by genus and differentia and a definition by a conjunction of constituent parts. But there is no mention of this requirement in this connection; and I should

[61] 1034b20–32, 1036b21–32.
[62] 998b4–6.
[63] 201c–210d; cf. also the discussion which follows the account of Socrates' dream (202–206), with its application of the problem of the relation between part and whole to the case of the constituent elements of the definition.
[64] *Met.* Δ25, 1023b22–4.
[65] *Met.* Δ24, 1023a35–6.
[66] *Met.* Δ24, 1023a36–7; Δ25, 1023b24–5.

argue that this is an indication of Aristotle's purpose in the *Topics*, which is to provide the disputant with such ammunition as will enable him to thrive in argument *as it is currently practised*. While this purpose does not preclude Aristotle from introducing concepts which have only been fully refined by his own analysis, yet it will result in the exclusion of arguments which have the effect of removing whole areas of propositions from the realm of permitted discourse: this would be the effect if the uniqueness requirement for definitions were enforced as a general principle for ordering the topics.

If we wish to determine the relation between the forms of definition considered in *Top.* Z13 and those which give the genus and differentia, the synonymity topic is of importance. This states the requirement that the whole and part should not be synonymous, and concludes from this that definitions which are of the form considered in Z13 should not contain elements which are synonymous with the definiendum.[67] Alexander[68] illustrates the topic with an example in which the genus is defined by a conjunction of its species. I have already noted that in *Met.* Δ25 Aristotle allows a sense in which the genus and differentia are parts of the species and another sense in which the species is part of the genus;[69] and this seems to confirm Alexander's interpretation. But this interpretation overlooks the implications of the fact that the genus and the species *are* synonymous.[70] If this topic is to be interpreted as applicable to the genus/differentia/species model of definition, its effect would be to exclude all mention of the genus in the definition, since the genus is synonymous with the species and yet, as a part, could not be so. So I conclude that this topic is not intended to cover the genus/differentia model of definition, and that the fact that this thesis about parts and wholes does not cover this model shows that caution must be exercised when we say that the genus and species are related in this way.

This conclusion is not at variance with the analysis of *Met.* Δ25. In *Met* Δ Aristotle is mainly concerned to mark off the various ways in which words may be used. The uses thus marked off are all legitimate uses; but the *circumstances* in which the words may be employed in their various usages may well be a matter for further analysis. Thus, at *Met.* Δ7, 1017a22–30, there is a mention of the variety of uses which characterise the word 'being' according to the different categories; but for a full account of how the word is properly used in each of the categories we must look further than *Met.* Δ7. Similar caution must be exercised over the comments in *Met* Δ25 about the use of the word 'part' in connection with

---

[67] 150b19–21.
[69] 1023b24–5.
[68] *In Topica* 490.6.
[70] *Top.* Δ3, 123a27–9; Δ6, 127b5–7.

universals. We may allow a sense to the assertion that a universal has parts either (a) because we recognise that a definite number of universals fall under it in such a way as between them to exhaust its extension, or (b) because we recognise that it can be analysed into more general universals which in combination define its nature alone. But if we accept this, we must also recognise the danger inherent in each of the two grounds for our assertion. These dangers are, in the case of (a), that the genus may be seen as an entity which exists in its own right and to which, because it is a whole, the parts are subordinate, and in the case of (b), that the species is seen as no more than a conjunction of the more general universals into which it can be dissolved by analysis. Aristotle regards these consequences as dangerous because of his conviction that it is in terms of the *infimae species* that the world is presented to our understanding: the individual is indefinable and unknowable,[71] and the more generic the universal, the more remote it is from reality.[72] This position is threatened by the misapprehensions which can accompany either of the grounds (a) or (b) for asserting that universals have parts; and for this reason we must be cautious about saying that universals have parts. When he denies at *Top.* Z13, 150b19–21, that the part can be synonymous with the whole, Aristotle is implicitly denying that the relations between genus and species should be described as those between parts and wholes. So although the synonymity topic is not intended to cover definitions of the genus/differentia model, it carries an implication for the theoretical basis of this model of definition.

Aristotle's comments on definitions in the form *these things*[73] have a further general bearing on his theory of definition. When we combine the observations of 150a15–21 on parts and wholes, with the particular lines of attack which are given in 150a2–14, as the structure of the whole section requires us to do, we can draw the conclusion that is implicit in the text: the 'subjects' (person *A* and person *B*) which can satisfy the criteria demanded by such definitions are *not* wholes with characteristics distinct from those of their parts (person *A*, person *B*). There is no guarantee that such 'subjects' possess any definite characteristics, since in some cases they possess both some characteristic and its contrary; and even in the case of the joint possession of a mina[74] it could be argued that, just as each possesses half a mina, so each lacks half a mina (i.e. the half which the other contributes to the joint fund), and so jointly they both possess and fail to possess a mina. Thus statements which

[71] *Met.* Z15, 1039b27–40a7.
[72] This is particularly clear in the argument of *Met.* Z12 that the most specific differentia is that which indicates the essence.
[73] 150a2–21.   [74] 150a8–9.

contain such multiple subjects offend the principle of non-contradiction, acceptance of which is argued in *Met.* Γ4 to be basic to meaningful discourse; and elsewhere Aristotle makes similar strictures on statements with multiple subjects.[75] However, definitions which are given in the form *these things* do nothing to prevent the substitution of the names of two distinct subjects for the name of the definiendum. But if the possibility of such substitution is not prevented, there will remain no justification for the claim that statements with multiple subjects are not unitary, since the notion of the unitary statement depends on that of the unitary term[76] and this notion in turn depends on that of the unity of the definiendum.[77]

It is important to be clear about the logical order of these theses. It may be objected, against the argument which I have developed from Aristotle's tactics in *Top.* Z13, that the principle of non-contradiction renders illegitimate *any* substitution of a plurality of things for the subject term in a statement: therefore Aristotle is not justified in offering persons A and B as 'a thing', and no significant point could be made via such malpractice. In a modern formal language, which would express a definition with such a formula as $\square$ (x) $(Fx{\rightarrow}Gx.Hx)$, the semantics of quantification would preclude a plural substitution for the variable.

But this objection mistakes the relation between definitions and the principle of non-contradiction. Formal languages depend on both for the proper use of quantification within them; and Aristotle relies heavily on the notion of definition to support the principle.[78] So at the most fundamental level the function of definitions is to provide us with unitary subjects of discourse. Aristotle is justified in using parts of logic which depend upon the fulfilment of this requirement, to show that certain kinds of definition are inadequate to their essential function.

One of the effects of the analysis in *Met.* Z10–12 of the *aporiai* which surround the notion of definition is to make it clear that the ideas about definition which are implicit in the dilemma of *Met.* B3, 998a21–998b14, stand in need of development. On the one hand, it is wrong to suppose that the definition should not contain mention of the constituent parts of the subject, although we must be clear about what the relevant constituent parts are.[79] On the other hand,

---

[75] *SE* 17, 176a12–13: 'discourse is demolished', of the demand that such questions as 'Are Koriskos and Kallias at home?' should be answered 'Yes' or 'No'; *De Int.* 8, 18a18–27, statements such as 'a man and a horse are neither true nor false'.

[76] *De Int.* 11, 20b12–15.

[77] Compare *De Int.* 20b15–19 with *Met.* Z12, 1037b12–18.

[78] *Met.* Γ4, 1006a28–1007b18.

[79] *Met.* Z10–11.

it is wrong to regard the genus and differentia as parts which *in conjunction* constitute the definition, since the unity which must characterise the definition will not result from such a conjunction.[80] In other words, Aristotle *agrees* with the thinkers of *Met.* B3, 998b4–8, in not allowing that the enumeration of constituent parts can constitute a definition; but he *criticises* them for (a) treating the elements of the definition as if they were constituent parts and (b) excluding from the elements of the definition (because they regard them merely as constituent parts) that which is essential to the nature of the definiendum. Despite their desire to escape from the notion of the whole as the sum of its parts, they are unable to do so, and the penalty which they pay for their failure is that they are forced to exclude from their definitions elements of the nature of the definiendum which are in fact essential to it. It is interesting to compare another argument from the discussion of definition in *Met.* Z where opponents' aspirations are shown to misfire in a similar way. In *Met.* Z15, Aristotle uses his thesis that individuals are indefinable to show that Plato's Forms cannot be objects of definition.[81] The Forms were, of course, postulated as objects of definition because Plato shared Aristotle's belief that individuals are indefinable. But by arguing that the Forms are as much individuals as the individuals which Plato regarded as indefinable, Aristotle shows that they lack precisely that characteristic – being objects of definition – which justifies their existence.

In the *Metaphysics* Aristotle uses the notions of matter and form, potentiality and actuality, to reinforce his conviction that the elements in the definition must fit together in such a way that the unity of the defined subject is not infringed.[82] In these discussions Aristotle tends to start from theses about the characteristics which must be possessed by the subject and to argue from these to conclusions about the nature of definition. Thus, in *Met.* Z12 he argues that the differentia should be divided by its own differentiae because only thus can the unity of the defined subject be preserved.[83] Not all the discussions in *Met.* Z follow this pattern: in the first part of Z4, for example, Aristotle uses considerations about the nature of definition to throw light on the notion of essence.[84] Generally, however, Aristotle argues from the facts of ontology to the correct way of reflecting them in language rather than *vice versa.* But in the *Topics* there is a suggestion of the reverse direction of argument. *Top.* Z13 provides two tests of a linguistic nature

[80] *Met.* Z12.　　　　　　　[81] 1040a8–1040b4.
[82] *Met.* Z12, H6.　　　　　[83] 1038a9–15.
[84] 1029b13–1030a28; cf. the concluding words of the section, 'now one should consider how one should *talk* about each thing, but not to a greater extent than how it *is* with that thing'.

which point in the same direction as the ontological arguments of *Met. Z.* Firstly, the synonymity topic[85] carries an implicit warning against regarding the elements of the definition as parts of a whole. Synonymity provides a linguistic test of whether the elements of the definition are parts of a whole (the definiendum). In *Top. Z*13 Aristotle uses it to test definitions which provide a conjunction of the parts of the subject; but its use can be extended to show that no definition which is simply a conjunction of parts can be satisfactory. For the definition must contain the genus, which *is* synonymous with the species. Secondly, the paradoxes which can be shown to result from definitions of the form *these things*[86] provide a linguistic indication of the need to ensure that the elements of the definition cannot exist in isolation from each other. An account of the relation between the elements of the definition must be provided which will indicate that the strictest unity obtains between them. We find such an account in *Met. Z*12 and H6, where the elements are said to be related as matter to form and potential to actual. But it is in *Top. Z*13 that the dangers of failing to provide this account become most apparent, when Aristotle shows that without it there is no check on the number of things which can combine to form a 'subject' which falls under the definition.

The unity of the definition: the threat of repetition

Similar considerations of method, as well as the same substantive issues in the theory of definition, arise in connection with the problems which surround *repetition* in statements. This phenomenon is discussed, always obscurely, in certain texts outside the *Topics*; but the contribution of *Top. Z* to the issue has received little attention.

In *Top. Z*3, 140b27–141a14, Aristotle examines the ways in which a definition can be attacked on the ground that it contains a repetition.[87] This fault in definition is one form of the more general fault of including more in the definition than is necessary;[88] and the examination of this general fault falls in turn under the more general heading of topics which examine whether the definition is 'proper'.[89] The fault of repetition, then, is one that relates to the linguistic form of the definition rather than to its success in indicating the subject's essence.[90]

The topic opens with an argument that such definitions as 'Desire is an appetite for the pleasant' are faulty because they generate repetition.[91] However, this argument is countered by consideration

[85] 150b19–21.   [86] 150a2–14.
[87] 'Saying the same thing more than once'.   [88] cf. Z3, 140a24.
[89] Z1, 139b12–18.   [90] cf. p. 110 above.
[91] 140b27–31.

of the case of the (unquestionably acceptable) definition of a Man as 'a biped footed animal'.[92] Finally, certain obviously repetitive definitions are considered.[93] My interest is with the first part of this discussion – 140b27–141a6. The repetition is generated from the proposed definition of Desire by using the proposition that desire is for the pleasant: if that which is the same as Desire (i.e. the proposed definition – an appetite for the pleasant) is also for the pleasant, then the definition of Desire will become 'appetite for the pleasant for the pleasant'.

The argument is compressed, but it can be given more fully as follows. If X is always A and if YZ is the definition of X, then (a) on every occasion XA can be substituted for X, and (b) on every occasion YZ can be substituted for X, and consequently (c) on every occasion YZA can be substituted for YZ. Therefore (by c) the definition of X can be expressed as YZA. But in the example considered in 140b27–31 the same symbol must be used for the A and the Y of our proof form; and thus in this case we derive the definition of X as YYZ. The example in 140b31–4 follows an exactly parallel course. Here for A (which equals Y) read 'biped', for Z read 'footed animal', and for YZ read 'biped footed animal': by making the substitutions of (a) and (b) we derive as a definition of Man: 'biped biped footed animal'. The purpose of this parallel example is to show how the moves which produced apparent paradox in the case of the definition of Desire as 'appetite for the pleasant' do not produce *real* paradox, since the same manoeuvres can be produced on the definition of Man as 'biped footed animal' and this latter definition is undoubtedly well-formed.[94]

But Aristotle is not content to rely simply on this argument from the parallel case; he seeks to show the false assumption in the manoeuvres which produced the apparent paradox. His comment is that in these cases we encounter nothing worse than repetition of the same word, whereas what is to be censured is the repeated making of the same predication.[95] He says that in the case of the definition of a Man 'biped is said concerning a biped footed animal', and comments that this is not the same as predicating the same thing of the same subject a second time. His reason for this appears to be that in the former case, the second occurrence of 'biped' merely repeats what is already in the predicate: in our symbolism,

[92] 140b31–141a6.
[93] 141a6–14.
[94] It may be objected that 'biped footed' is itself repetitious. On this point see *PA* A2, 642b7–10, disarmed by *Met.* Z12, 1038a9–33 (for this text see pp. 121–2 above). But the context in the *Topics* from which I have taken this example is not concerned with this apparent difficulty, but rather with the surface repetition of the single word 'biped'.
[95] 141a4–6.

the Y in the YZ of which a further Y appears to be predicated, is itself a predicate and not a subject of predication. But the fault of repetition *would* occur if 'biped' were predicated of a footed animal – i.e. if Y were predicated of Z.[96] For in such a case YZ could on every occasion be substituted for Z, and thus the definition of X as YZ could be converted into YYZ. The difference between the two cases, one innocent and one vicious, can be seen from the following:

(1) (innocent)   (a) X equals YZ (2) (vicious)   (a) X equals YZ
             (b) X equals YX (b) Z equals YZ
   therefore   (c) X equals YYZ therefore   (c) X equals YYZ

In these two cases premiss (a) represents the definition and (b) the possibility of substitution established by the predication, while (c) represents the conclusion which can be derived from these premisses by substitution. It will be seen that in both (1) and (2) premiss (a) and conclusion (c) are the same; on the other hand, premiss (b) is different in the two proofs. In proof (1) the argument depends on the conjunction of two premisses each of which predicates the same thing – Y – of X; but in proof (2) the argument does *not* depend on twice predicating the same thing of the same thing, i.e. on duplicating the *same act of predication*, but rather on the combination of the predication of Y of X (in a) and of Y of Z (in b). Since by the transitivity rule[97] whatever is predicated of the genus (Z in our proof form) must also be predicated of the species (X), premiss (b) in proof (2) constitutes a second, *distinct* occurrence of the same predication. That this is the correct interpretation of Aristotle's distinction between 'saying the same word twice' and 'making the same predication twice' is confirmed by the examples which are given in 141a6–14 to illustrate the latter fault, all of which consist of defining expressions in which term Z imports term Y in such a way that the expression YZ can be expanded into YYZ.

Aristotle says elsewhere that the differentia cannot be predicated of the genus[98] and that the genus cannot be predicated of the differentia.[99] The first of these theses is derived from his conviction that the genus is of wider extension than the differentia, and that consequently not all of the things which fall under the genus are also characterised by the differentia. It is turned against the Academy, in their capacity as upholders of the doctrine of Ideas, at *Top.* Z6, 143b11–32. Here it is argued that where we have a genus which is divided by a positive and a privative differentia (e.g. A Length divided by With Breadth and Without Breadth), the

---

[96] cf. 140b35–7.
[97] *Top.* Δ2, 122a3–7, 122a31–122b17.
[98] *Top.* Z6, 144a28–31; *Top.* Δ2, 123a6–10; *Met.* B3, 998b23–7.
[99] *Top.* Z6, 144a31–b3; Δ2, 122b20–4.

genus A Length (which, as Aristotle interprets the Academic position, is *some individual* length) must by the principle of non-
contradiction, either have or not have breadth and thus must take
one of its differentiae as a predicate:[100] that is to say, the function
of the Form as genus is inconsistent with its nature as a self-
subsistent entity. In the case of this thesis, then, we appear to have
a line of argument against the view that the differentia can be
predicated of the genus, which is independent of the repetition topic
of Z3. However, in the case of the second thesis of Z6, 144a28–
144b3, that the genus cannot be predicated of the differentia, the
argument is similar to that of the repetition topic. Aristotle says[101]
that were the genus predicated of the differentia, rather than being
predicated of that of which the differentia is predicated (i.e. the
species), 'many animals would be predicated of the species, because
the differentiae are predicated of the species'. The situation to
which this comment alludes is exactly the same as that which is
spelled out in the repetition topic, although the model is more
extended. If the definition of X is ABC, of which A represents genus
and B and C represent differentiae, A will be predicated of B and of
C and so will be predicated twice of X (three times if we include
the explicit predication of A as genus).

We have already seen that a feature of Aristotle's method in the
Topics is to use certain conceptual considerations to make what on
the surface are points of rather local and limited interest; but when
we bring in comparable texts from other works, these considerations
are seen to play a crucial part in the support of Aristotle's theory of
definition against rival theories. The use of the repetition topic in
Top. Z6 is an example of this. In Aristotle's view Plato's conception
of the elements in the definition as independent, self-subsisting
entities (Forms) leads to intolerable difficulties. For the differentia
Biped will be something which is biped, – that is, an animal; and
the genus *an animal* will be an individual animal with, among other
characteristics, some definite number of feet. Therefore the genus
will be predicated of the differentia and the differentia of the genus.
This is unacceptable to Aristotle, who views the genus and the
differentia as mutually complementary elements of something
different in kind from them.

So while the arguments of *Top.* Z6, 143b11–32, and Δ2, 123a6–
10, point to an inconsistency between Plato's ontology and his
definition procedure and can, in the case of *certain* differentiae,
produce radical paradox, the repetition topic produces insight into
the essential nature of what Aristotle believed to be the characteristic error in the Platonic ontology of the definition. For it shows
that within the terms of this ontology to give a definition is not to

[100] 143b21–3. [101] 144a36–8.

make a single, linguistically complex, predication but to make the same predication twice. Where two Forms are combined, as genus and differentia, to form a definition, each of the Forms will be characterised by the other. So, by using the substitution manoeuvre which the repetition topic exploits, it will be possible to show, in the case of both the genus and the differentia, that the same predication is being made twice: it is made both explicitly and, because each of the predicates entails the other, implicitly. The absurdity of the repetition is a very potent indicator of the absurdity of the ontology which makes the repetition possible.

It may be thought that my analysis of Aristotle's argument in *Top.* Z3 for condemning certain combinations of premisses as productive of vicious repetition (i.e. that combination of premisses which satisfies proof form (2) above) would commit him to rejecting something which elsewhere he asserts. For if repetition arises in the case in which we predicate the same thing both of the subject of definition and of an element in the definition, Aristotle's rule that the genus of the genus in the definition can be predicated *both* of the genus in the definition *and* of the subject of the definition[102] would seem to be as generative of repetition as the views which in the preceding paragraph we have just seen him condemn. For example, if one can predicate Substance of both a Man and an Animal, the characterisation of a Man as an Animal Substance will generate the repetitive characterisation of a Man as an Animal Substance Substance. However, if such an application can indeed be made of Aristotle's argument, his own examples of vicious repetition in Z3, 141a6–14, show him curiously unaware of it, since one of these examples certainly combines a more and a less generic element in the nature of the subject.[103] Moreover in *De Int.* 11, 21a16–18, he argues that a single predication cannot be formed from the combination of two predicates, each of which is separately true of the subject, when one has the other as an element in its definition.[104] This prohibition follows a rather compressed rehearsal of the repetition paradoxes that can arise if it is supposed that predicates which are related in this way can be combined.[105] Aristotle gives as examples of combined predicates which generate repetition, 'Socrates is a Socrates man', which is derived from 'Socrates is Socrates' and 'Socrates is a man', and 'a man is a biped man', which is derived from 'a man is a man' and 'a man is biped'.[106] These generate repetition because for the second occurrence of 'a man' in 'a man is a biped man' it is possible to substitute 'biped man', given that 'a man is a biped man', and thus 'a man is

---

[102] *Top.* Δ2, 122a3–7. [103] 141a6–9.
[104] cf. Ross, *Analytics*, p. 582 *ad* 84a13.
[105] 20b31–21a4. [106] 21a2–3.

a biped man' becomes 'a man is a biped biped man'.[107] In *De Int.*
11, then, Aristotle uses the argument from repetition to rule that a
single predication cannot be formed from two predicates one of
which occurs in the definition of the other. So the argument of this
chapter does *not* reject the belief, from which this discussion started,
that of the species can be predicated both its genus and the genus
of that genus; but it *does* reject the belief that a single predication
can be formed from the predication of these two genera. Since the
definition must be unitary, it cannot consist of two predicates the
combined predication of which does not constitute a single predication, whether these uncombinable predicates are linked by the word
'and' as in *Top.* Z3[108] or not.[109] This accords with Aristotle's view
in the *Topics* that the predicates (the generic and the differentiating)
which in combination form the definition, are *not* predicated of
each other, and so they can in combination constitute the unitary
predication which the definition must be.

Two texts from the *SE* are important if we wish to understand
the nature of the repetition regresses and their influence on Aristotle's thought. *SE* 13 and 31 deal respectively with the means of
inducing an opponent and of avoiding an opponent's inducement to
repeat the same thing, a fault which Aristotle calls *adoleschein* –
'chattering'.[110] This word occurs in Plato several times as a term of
disparagement upon unserious intellectuals;[111] but nowhere is it
linked with the notion of vicious regress in argument. It is noteworthy that Aristotle feels it necessary to explain what fault he
means by the word.[112] On the other hand the vice of the infinite
regress receives a classic illustration in the Third Man argument
which greatly impressed Aristotle; and his frequent use of the appeal
to an infinite regress to refute a thesis[113] confirms the impression
given by the *Topics* and the *SE* that the fault was recognised by
others.

[107] cf. the example of 'a man is a white man' in 20b37–40. 'Again if white,
the whole thing as well' does not mean that the predicate 'white' imports
'white man', since this would yield the repetition 'a man is a white *man*
man' rather than 'a man is a white *white* man' (20b40). Rather it means
that, on the view that separate predications can be combined, the predication of 'white' of a man justifies predicating 'a white man' of a man, so
that for 'a man' in the predicate we can substitute 'a white man' to give
the repetitive predicate 'a white white man'.
[108] 141a7, 16, 20.
[109] *De Int.* 11, 21a3–4, 17; *Top.* 141a10.
[110] *SE* 13, 173a32; 3, 165b15–17; *Top.* E2, 130a34; Θ2, 158a27–8.
[111] *Pol.* 299b; *Theaet.* 195b–195c; *Soph.* 225d; *Rep.* 488e; *Phaedo* 70c.
The use of the word at *Crat.* 401b and *Phaedr.* 270a, while superficially
commendatory, seems in fact to be ironical.
[112] *SE* 3, 165b15–17.
[113] cf. Bonitz, *Index* 74b41–57.

SE 13 presents some cases where the repetition regress is generated in the same way as occurs in *Top.* Z3 and *De Int.* 11: from the premises that X equals YZ and that X equals XY (or that there is an XY) it can be derived that X equals YYZ (or that there is an YYZ).[114] Aristotle comments that such regresses can occur in the case either (*a*) of things which are themselves relative and have relative things for a genus and are correlative with the same thing as that with which their genus is correlative, or (*b*) of things in whose definitions are included the subject of which they are predicated.[115] Examples of (*a*) are Double, Desire; examples of (*b*) are Odd and Snub. After indicating how the paradoxes can be generated, Aristotle hints at the solution which he will give in *SE* 31 when he says[116] that the paradoxes arise from failure to consider whether the problematic terms mean the same thing when they stand in isolation as when they are combined with other terms. This idea is developed in *SE* 31. In the case of relative things we must not regard the predication of the relative in isolation from its correlative as meaning the same as its predication together with its correlative, if indeed the isolated predication has any meaning; nor should we regard the relative term as having the same meaning when used generally as when it is specified, since the correlatives of the general and of the specific relative things are different.[117] In the case of things whose definitions include that of which they are predicates we must maintain that the term for the attribute in isolation from the subject does not mean the same as when it is combined with a subject: both noses and legs have the attribute of being concave but 'concave nose' means 'snub' (not 'bandy') 'nose' and 'concave legs' means 'bandy' (not 'snub') 'legs'.[118]

It will be useful to examine these prescriptions both for their value in countering the manoeuvres which generate repetition and for the light which they may throw on Aristotle's theory of predication.

(1) 181b26–34: that a relative term does not mean the same when it is predicated in isolation from its correlative as when it is combined with it. This provision is designed to preclude the initial move which by itself generates one form of repetition regress, the move from 'X equals XY'[119] to 'X equals XYY' etc.: the sense of 'double'

---

[114] The texture of the examples varies. 173a35–8 uses only two terms, 173a39–40 uses three, while 173b8–11 differs from both the previous examples in producing an entity which is designated by a repetitive expression rather than in producing a repetitive predicate for a subject. But in all cases the logical manoeuvres follow the same pattern.

[115] 173b1–8. [116] 173b11–16.
[117] 181b25–35. [118] 181b35–182a3.
[119] e.g. Double equals Double of Half, 173a35.

in which it can stand in isolation, and thereby supposedly take as its substitute 'double of half', is distinct from that which it bears in 'double of half'. As to the more general force of this comment, G. E. L. Owen[120] has well argued that Aristotle's stipulation here is to be taken in conjunction with his attack in the *Peri Ideōn* [121] on the Academic conflation of what are for Aristotle the irreducibly distinct notions of substance and relative thing. Aristotle defines a relative thing as that for which to be is to stand in relation to something else;[122] and this view is fully reflected in his comment in *SE* 31 that relatives which are predicated in isolation either mean nothing or (charitably to the Academy) something different from when they are predicated in the way in which Aristotle believes that *relatives* ought to be predicated.

(2) 181b34–5: that a relative does not mean the same when it is predicated in a general form as when it assumes a specific form of that general kind: 'skill' *tout court* does not mean the same as 'skill' in 'medical skill'. The ground for this obscure statement is to be sought in Aristotle's belief that the *meaning* of a relative essentially involves its correlative, e.g. 'double' *means* 'double of half', and in his belief that the correlatives of the genus and the species are distinct.[123] Once again Aristotle's provision here has the effect of blocking the regress. It will be remembered that the form of the regress was: (1) X equals XY (because X is Y), (2) X equals YZ, therefore (3) X equals YYZ. The regress can be produced by someone who supposes that because both Y and Z are predicated of X, these elements can with equal propriety, and therefore with equal justification of substitution, be combined into the predicates XY and YZ. The effect of Aristotle's provision in 181b34–5 is to show that these combined predicates are very different in character and that the substitutions which occur in the regress arguments are *not* justified; in particular, the substitution of YZ for X in XY is not to be allowed. This accords with the views of *Top.* Z and *De Int.* 11 which we have already considered. For, (*a*) we may say that X is Y but must not combine X and Y into a single predication, since Y as correlative of X is included in the definition of X; and (*b*) we may *not* say that Z is Y but *may* combine Z and Y into a single predication, since YZ is the definition of X. The thesis that the logical behaviour of the relative genus and its species is distinct is put to important use in the argument of *Cat.* 8, 11a20–38, that in some cases the species is relative 'in respect of its genus' but not 'in respect

---

[120] 'Dialectic and Eristic in the treatment of the Forms', pp. 113–15.
[121] Fr. 3 (Ross, *Fragmenta*) = Alexander *in Metaphysica* 83, 22–30.
[122] *Cat.* 7, 8a31–2; *Top.* Z4, 142a29.
[123] *Top.* Z9, 147a23–8; Δ4, 125a25–32. In some cases the species of a relative genus is not itself relative, *Top.* Δ4, 124b15–22; *Cat.* 8, 11a20–38.

of itself'.[124] Knowledge is of something, whereas medical knowledge is not, in itself, of something; rather, medical knowledge is *knowledge* (the genus) of something.[125] In this case there is a relative genus whose species is not relative in respect of itself; but, as the analysis of *SE* 31 shows, the distinction between that to which the genus is essentially related and that to which the species is related in respect of the genus is important when we consider cases where both the species and the genus *are* relative, as is the case with Desire and Appetite.

(3) 181b35–182a3: that a predicate does not mean the same in isolation from a subject as when it is combined with it. The effect of this provision is similar to that treated under (2). In the example of 'snub', 'snub nose' and 'concave nose' are said to mean the same; consequently, to substitute 'concave *nose*' for 'snub' in 'snub nose' is illegitimate. In symbols the regress ran: (1) there is an XY ('X' stands for 'snub', 'Y' for 'nose'), (2) X is YZ ('Z' stands for 'concave'), therefore (3) there is an YYZ. Against this Aristotle insists that XY means the same as YZ and that to suppose that YZ can be substituted for the X in XY rather than for the whole expression is to overlook this fact. It is true that Z means something other than X, so that the combination of Z and Y is needed to establish the meaning of X. But this does not authorise us to substitute YZ for *part* of an expression to the *whole* of which it is equivalent in meaning. The question of how 'snub' is to be construed, and therefore of what it is to be snub, is a matter of general importance. For as Aristotle says at *Met.* E1, 1025b34–5, 'all natural things are spoken of in the same way as what is snub', because everything which is studied by natural philosophy (*phusikē*) is a compound of matter (the nose) and form (the concavity).[126] In *Met.* Z5 Aristotle considers whether such things as Snub Nose can have definitions.[127] One part of his argument focusses attention on the definition – 'a snub nose' – which such a thing as a snub nose would have, and the repetition regress is reproduced.[128] The regress follows a similar course to that of *SE* 13; but on this occasion the answer of *SE* 31 will not be applicable, since *the definition itself* contains elements which are predicated of each other ('snub' of 'nose'). The argu-

---

124 The terminology of *Top.* Δ4, 124b23–7, rather than of *Cat.* 8; but the distinction made in the two passages is the same.

125 *Cat.* 11a24–32.

126 For a clear case of a natural substance which follows the logic of 'snub', cf. the analysis of blood at *PA* B2, 649a13–17; B3, 649b20–7, as a compound of heat and a substratum which is not intrinsically hot.

127 Not Snubness, as Ross, *Metaphysics*, vol. 2, p. 173–4, supposes. Snubness is effectively defined at 1030b31–2, and as an example of a 'combined thing' we have Odd Number, not Oddness, at 1031a6.

128 1030b28–36.

ments of *SE* 31 are designed to preserve the possibility of making certain predications (e.g. 'snub', 'double', 'for pleasure') from the threat which is held out by the repetition regresses. In this way it is shown that we can predicate 'snub' of a nose without producing paradox. But this does not have the result that these elements can combine to form the complete unity that a definition is required to be. As with conjoined predicates, so here this basic requirement upon definitions is used in *De Int.* 11 to generate the repetitions which show that certain combinations of predicates cannot constitute a single predication. They cannot therefore be what definitions must be. 'A Snub Nose' is an example of such a combination, since 'nose' forms part of the definition of snub; and use is made of the repetition regress of *SE* 13 to show that 'a Snub Nose' is not a well-formed definition. From this in turn it is inferred that such things as a snub nose cannot have an essence or a definition or, if they do, it is only in a secondary and qualified sense.[129]

It is useful to conduct this review of the passages outside the *Topics* where the repetition regresses are discussed, because only when it is seen in this larger context can the importance of the discussion of repetitive definitions in *Top. Z*3 be appreciated. Aristotle starts from the position, whether inherited from others or not, that to say something which generates repetition is a vice in discourse. This condemnation can be rationalised by appeal to the fact that someone who repeats himself does not say *some* (i.e. *one*) thing;[130] and while repetition is to be avoided in all forms of discourse, in giving a definition one must be specially on guard against committing this fault because to define is essentially to say *one* thing. Recognition of this vice, then, is important; but we must also be on guard against an argument which would prove that *all* definitions exhibit this vice. Such an argument is that which Aristotle gives in *Top. Z*3, 140b31–4, and I have discussed his solution to it.[131] It is vital to this solution that the elements of the definition be not predicated of each other, and the main contribution of the discussion of the repetition regresses to the theory of definition is to reinforce this view of the relation between the elements of the definition. The importance of the discussions in the *SE* is twofold. Firstly by showing in greater detail than *Top. Z*3 how to escape the arguments which produce the repetition regress, they incidentally show how to preserve from attack the definitions which serve as premises for the regress arguments.[132] Secondly, by their analysis of

[129] *Met. Z*5, 1031a7–14.
[130] cf. Plato *Soph.* 237d6–7.
[131] pp. 124–5 above.
[132] Such definitions as e.g. 'Desire is Appetite For Pleasure', 173a39; 'Snubness is Concavity Of The Nose', 173b10.

the fallacies involved in the reasoning which produces the repetition, they clarify the nature of the distinction between those definitions which do generate repetition and those which do not. If we revert to the symbols already used – X is the subject, Y the differentia, Z the genus – this point can be made as follows: (1) Y and Z may not be predicated of each other but they may combine to form a single predicate (the definition); (2) Y may be predicated of X (e.g. biped of man) or X may be predicated of Y (e.g. snub of nose), but X and Y may not combine to form a single predication, especially not to form the definition;[133] (3) in those cases where the attempt is made to predicate Y of Z (e.g. for pleasure of appetite) or Z of Y (e.g. concave of nose) *either* this is to be condemned according to thesis (1) *or* we may say that what is really occurring in such predications is that Y or Z is being predicated of X, since YZ designates the same thing as YX and ZY the same as ZX. It is in respect of thesis (3) that *SE* 31 is most helpful in the understanding of *Top.* Z3. For it brings out clearly the manner in which the innocent combination of premisses, given as proof (1) on p. 125 above, differs from the vicious, given as proof (2). If we can reduce a case of the predication of Y of Z or of Z of Y, which gives rise to premiss (b) of the vicious proof (2), to a case of the predication of Y or Z of X, we have an instance of proof (1); and this, as I argued on p. 125, does not amount to a double predication of the same thing.

In the examination of the texts which present the repetition regresses we have followed Aristotle's practice of shifting between the formal and the material modes of presenting the case, between the mentions and uses of the words involved. Bewildered by this, some who are unfamiliar with his discussions may suppose that his difficulties are to be resolved simply by drawing attention to these shifts. But while this criticism cannot be sustained in detail, it also fails on a general level to grasp what method needs to be followed over definitions. Definitions represent *things* in *words*; and Aristotle's approach to the problems does not ignore this dual aspect of the situation. It is characteristic, as we have seen, of dialectic to approach things through the forms of words in which they are portrayed. In the case of the repetition regresses we find this dialectical method used not only in the logical works but also in the *Metaphysics*, because dialectic has a special role in the investigation of definitions.[134] So we should not be surprised to find that in these

---

[133] I have argued that the clue to the interpretation of *Met.* Z5 lies in recognising thesis (2).

[134] *Top.* A2, 101a36–101b4; for a fuller discussion of this see chapter two above.

contexts Aristotle, who resisted the notion of a meta-language,[135] frequently mentions words to explore their use.

Summary: the Topics on definition

In the preceding discussions I have examined various problems of definition to which the *Topics* makes its contribution, and also the peculiar character of that contribution. There are two general features of Aristotle's theory of definition which have been prominent; these are the requirements that the definition be (*a*) unitary and (*b*) unique. The first requirement dominates the discussion of definition in *Met.* Z–H, especially Z4–6, 12, 17, and H6. The second is less in evidence, but it lies behind the discussion in *Met.* Z10–11 of the elements of the definition.

These requirements receive little explicit mention in the *Topics*, although the uniqueness requirement is used in the proof that the definition must be by elements which are prior and absolutely more intelligible than the subject[136] and is alluded to in the argument that it is possible to establish definitions.[137] But, I have argued, indirectly the *Topics* advances considerations which are relevant to both of them. The arguments which relate to the elements of the definition and to the repetition regresses, reinforce the need to give an account of the nature of a definition which will show that its elements combine to form a unity in the strictest sense. The topics for dealing with definitions in the form of conjunctions carry clear warning of the dangers which can attend such a form of definition; and insofar as one topic – that of synonymity – which is recommended for dealing with such definitions, could be used to upset any definition of the genus/differentia form, the discussion points to the need to settle which is to be *the* form of definition. Perhaps neither of the forms of definition is in itself fully adequate; but it is clear that it is not possible for both of them to stand.

In these ways the *Topics* supports the theory of definition as it is expounded in the *Metaphysics*. It does so by advancing considerations which constitute common ground for Aristotle and his contemporaries, and which do not depend for their acceptance on novel and controversial theses of Aristotle's own devising. His analysis of the elements of the definition embodies features which were present in others' thought, but effects a synthesis which had apparently eluded others. His comments on definitions in conjunction form

---

[135] See my 'The codification of false refutations in Aristotle's *De Sophisticis Elenchis*', p. 51.

[136] *Top.* Z4, 141a35; cf. p. 113–14 above.

[137] *Top.* H3, 153a15–22: 'the elements of the definition must be the *only* things which are predicated of the subject as part of its nature'.

provide easily accessible linguistic indicators of the difficulties which can ensue if the form of the definition makes it possible for the definition to be satisfied by a plurality of subjects. The repetition regresses show clearly the error in regarding the elements of definition as capable of existing in isolation each from the other. In all these cases the *Topics* provides a detailed illustration of the method according to which we start from what is intelligible to someone and move from this to what is intelligible absolutely in such a way that he too finds it intelligible.

BIBLIOGRAPHY

Ackrill, J. L., *Aristotle's Categories and De Interpretatione*, Oxford, 1963.
Alexander Aphrodisiensis, *In Aristotelis Metaphysica Commentaria*, ed. M. Hayduck, Berlin, 1891.
Alexander Aphrodisiensis, *In Aristotelis Topicorum Libros Octo Commentaria*, ed. M. Wallies, Berlin, 1891.
Allen, R. E., 'Forms and Standards', *Philosophical Quarterly* 9 (1959), 164–7.
Anscombe, G. E. M., 'The Intentionality of Sensation', in *Analytical Philosophy: Second Series*, ed. R. J. Butler, Oxford, 1965.
Arnim, H. von, 'Das Ethische in Aristoteles' Topika', *Anzeiger der Akademie der Wissenschaften in Wien* 63 (1926), 151–7.
Arpe, C., *Das τί ἦν εἶναι bei Aristoteles*, Hamburg, 1938.
Austin, J. L., 'Are There A Priori Concepts?', in *Philosophical Papers*, ed. J. O. Urmson and G. J. Warnock, Oxford, 1961.
Balme, D. M., 'Aristotle's use of differentiae in Zoology', in *Aristote et Les Problèmes de Méthode*, Louvain–Paris, 1961.
Balme, D. M., 'Γένος and Εἶδος in Aristotle's Biology', *Classical Quarterly* NS 12 (1962), 81–98.
Bambrough, J. R., 'Aristotle on Justice: A Paradigm of Philosophy', in *New Essays on Plato and Aristotle*, ed. J. R. Bambrough, London, 1965.
Bambrough, J. R., 'Principia Metaphysica', *Philosophy* 39 (1964), 97–109.
Bambrough, J. R., 'Unanswerable Questions', *Aristotelian Society: Supplementary Volume* 40 (1966), 151–72.
Bambrough, J. R., 'Universals and Family Resemblances', *Proceedings of the Aristotelian Society* NS 61 (1960–1), 207–22.
Black, M., 'Probability', in *The Encyclopedia Of Philosophy* 6, 464–79, New York, 1967.
Bonitz, H., *Aristotelis Metaphysica*, Berlin, 1848–9.
Bonitz, H., *Aristotelische Studien* IV, Vienna, 1866.
Bonitz, H., *Index Aristotelicus*, Berlin, 1870.
Braun, E., *Zur Einheit der aristotelischen 'Topik'*, Inaugural-Dissertation, Spich Bez. Köln, 1959.
Brunschwig, J., *Aristotle Topiques, Tome I (Livres I–IV)*, Budé Series, Paris, 1967.
Caizzi, F. D., *Antisthenis Fragmenta*, Varese–Milano, 1966.
Charlton, W. E., *Aristotle's Physics Books I and II*, Oxford, 1970.
Cherniss, H., *Aristotle's Criticism of Plato and the Academy* vol 1, Baltimore, 1944.
Cherniss, H., 'The Relation of the *Timaeus* to Plato's Later Dialogues',

American Journal of Philosophy 78 (1957), 225–66.

Cherniss, H., *The Riddle of the Early Academy*, California, 1945.

Chroust, A.-H., 'The First Thirty Years of Modern Aristotelian Scholarship', *Classica et Mediaevalia* 24 (1963), 27–57.

Colli, G., *Aristotele: Organon*, Turin, 1955.

Cornford, F. M., 'Mathematics and Dialectic in The *Republic* VI–VII', *Mind* 41 (1932), 37–52 and 173–90.

de Pater, W. A., *Les Topiques d'Aristotle et la Dialectique Platonicienne*, Fribourg, 1965.

Dirlmeier, F., 'Zum gegenwärtigen Stand der Aristoteles-Forschung', *Wiener Studien* 76 (1963), 52–67.

Diels, H. and Kranz, W., *Die Fragmente der Vorsokratiker*, 11th edn, Berlin, 1964.

Düring, I., *Aristoteles – Darstellung und Interpretation seines Denkens*, Heidelberg, 1966.

Düring, I., 'Aristotle's Use of Examples in the *Topics*', in *Aristotle on Dialectic – The Topics*, ed. G. E. L. Owen, Oxford, 1968.

Ebbinghaus, K., *Ein formales Modell der Syllogistik des Aristoteles*, Göttingen, 1965.

Evans, J. D. G., 'Aristotle on Relativism', *Philosophical Quarterly* 24 (1974), 193–203.

Evans, J. D. G., 'The codification of false refutations in Aristotle's *De Sophisticis Elenchis*', *Proceedings of the Cambridge Philological Society* NS 21 (1975), 42–52.

Forster, E. S., *Aristotle, On Sophistical Refutations*, Loeb Translation, London, 1955.

Frege, G., *Philosophical Writings*, transl. P. T. Geach and M. Black, Oxford, 1960.

Gallop, D., *Plato Phaedo*, Oxford, 1975.

Geach, P. T., 'Aristotle on Conjunctive Propositions', *Ratio* 5 (1963), 33–45.

Geach, P. T., 'The Third Man Again', *Philosophical Review* 65 (1956), 72–82.

Geach, P. T. and Anscombe, G. E. M., *Three Philosophers*, Oxford, 1963.

Gohlke, P., 'Untersuchungen zur *Topik* des Aristoteles', *Hermes* 63 (1928), 457–79.

Grimaldi, W. M. A., 'The Aristotelian *Topics*', *Traditio* 14 (1958), 1–16.

Grote, G., *Aristotle*, ed. A. Bain and G. C. Robertson, London, 1880.

Gulley, N., *The Philosophy of Socrates*, London, 1968.

Guthrie, W. K. C., *A History of Greek Philosophy* vols 1, 2, Cambridge, 1962–5.

Guthrie, W. K. C., 'Aristotle as a Historian of Philosophy: Some Preliminaries', *Journal of Hellenic Studies* 77 (Part 1) (1957), 35–41.

Guthrie, W. K. C., 'The Development of Aristotle's Theology', *Classical Quarterly* 27 (1933), 162–71, and 28 (1934), 90–8.

Hambruch, E., *Logische Regeln der platonischen Schule in der aristotelischen Topik*, Berlin, 1904.

Hardie, W. F. R., *Aristotle's Ethical Theory*, Oxford, 1968.

Hicken, W., 'The Character and Provenance of Socrates' Dream in the

Theaetetus', *Phronesis* 3 (1958), 126–45.

Hinitikka, J., *Time and Necessity*, Oxford, 1973.

Huby, P. M., 'The Date of Aristotle's *Topics* and its Treatment of the Theory of Ideas', *Classical Quarterly* NS 12 (1962), 72–80.

Husik, I., 'On the *Categories* of Aristotle', *Philosophical Review* 13 (1904), 514–28.

Jaeger, W., *Aristotle – Fundamentals of the History of His Development*, transl. R. Robinson, Oxford, 1948.

Jaeger, W., *Scripta Minora*, Rome, 1960.

Kapp, E., 'Syllogistik', in *Real-Encyclopädie der classischen Altertumswissenschaft* 2 Reihe IV 1 (1931), 1046–67.

Kapp, E., *Greek Foundations of Traditional Logic*, New York, 1942.

Kirwan, C., *Aristotle's Metaphysics, Books* Γ, Δ, E, Oxford, 1971.

Kirwan, C., 'Plato and relativity', *Phronesis* 19 (1974), 112–29.

Kneale, W. and M., *The Development of Logic*, Oxford, 1962.

Lang, P., *De Speusippi Academici Scriptis – Accedunt Fragmenta*, Bonn, 1911.

Le Blond, J. M., *Eulogos et L'Argument de Convenance chez Aristote*, Paris, 1938.

Le Blond, J. M., 'La définition chez Aristote', *Gregorianum* 20 (1939), 351–80.

Le Blond, J. M., *Logique et Méthode chez Aristote*, Paris, 1939.

Lloyd, A. C., 'Aristotle's Categories Today', *Philosophical Quarterly* 16 (1966), 258–67.

Lloyd, A. C., 'Genus, Species and Ordered Series in Aristotle', *Phronesis* 7 (1962), 67–90.

Lloyd, A. C., 'Plato's Description of Division', *Classical Quarterly* NS 2 (1952), 105–12.

Lloyd, G. E. R., 'The Development of Aristotle's Theory of the Classification of Animals', *Phronesis* 6 (1961), 59–81.

Mackie, J. L., 'Self-Refutation – A Formal Analysis', *Philosophical Quarterly* 14 (1964), 193–203.

Maier, H., *Die Syllogistik des Aristoteles*, Tübingen, 1896–1900.

Mansion, A., 'L'origine du syllogisme et la théorie de la science chez Aristote', in *Aristote et Les Problèmes de Méthode*, Louvain–Paris, 1961.

Mansion, A., 'Philosophie première, philosophie seconde, et métaphysique chez Aristote', *Revue Philosophique De Louvain* 56 (1958), 165–221.

Moraux, P., 'La joute dialectique d'après le huitième livre des *Topiques*', in *Aristotle on Dialectic – The Topics*, ed. G. E. L. Owen, Oxford, 1968.

Moraux, P., 'La méthode d'Aristote dans l'étude du ciel (*De Caelo* I 1 – II 12)', in *Aristote et Les Probèmes de Méthode*, Louvain–Paris, 1961.

Moser, S., *Zur Lehre von der Definition bei Aristoteles* Part 1, Innsbruck, 1935.

Owen, G. E. L., 'A Proof in the Περὶ Ἰδεῶν', *Journal of Hellenic Studies* 77 (Part 1) (1957), 103–11.

Owen, G. E. L., ed. *Aristotle on Dialectic – The Topics*, Oxford, 1968.

Owen, G. E. L., 'Dialectic and Eristic in the Treatment of the Forms', in *Aristotle on Dialectic – The Topics*, ed. G. E. L. Owen, Oxford, 1968.

Owen, G. E. L., 'Logic and metaphysics in some earlier works of Aristotle', in *Aristotle and Plato in the Mid-Fourth Century*, ed. I. Düring and G. E. L. Owen, Göteborg, 1960.

Owen, G. E. L., *The Platonism of Aristotle*, Dawes Hicks Lecture on Philosophy, British Academy, 1965.

Owen, G. E. L., 'Τιθέναι τὰ φαινόμενα', in *Aristote et Les Problèmes de Méthode*, Louvain–Paris, 1961.

Owens, J., *The Doctrine of Being in the Aristotelian Metaphysics*, Toronto, 1957.

Pacius, J., *Aristotelis Stagiritae Peripateticorum Principis Organum*, Frankfurt, 1597.

Patzig, G., 'Aristotle and Syllogisms from False Premisses', *Mind* 68 (1959), 186–92.

Patzig, G., *Die aristotelische Syllogistik*, Göttingen, 1963.

Patzig, G., 'Theologie und Ontologie in der "Metaphysik" des Aristoteles', *Kant-Studien* 52 (1960–1), 185–205.

Peck, A. L., 'Plato's *Parmenides*: some suggestions for its interpretation', *Classical Quarterly* NS 3 (1953), 126–50, and NS 4 (1954), 31–45.

Philippson, R., 'Il Frammento Logico Fiorentino', *Rivista di Filologia* NS 7 (1929), 495–506.

Pickard-Cambridge, W. A., 'Topica and De Sophisticis Elenchis', in *The Works of Aristotle* translated into English under the editorship of Sir David Ross, Oxford, 1928.

Poste, E., *Aristotle On Fallacies or The Sophistici Elenchi*, London, 1866.

Rackham, H., *Aristotle, Eudemian Ethics*, Loeb translation, London, 1935.

Robinson, R., *Definition*, Oxford, 1950.

Robinson, R., *Plato's Earlier Dialectic*, Oxford, 1953.

Ross, W. D., *Aristotelis Fragmenta Selecta*, Oxford, 1955.

Ross, W. D., *Aristotle's Metaphysics*, Oxford, 1924.

Ross, W. D., *Aristotle's Physics*, Oxford, 1936.

Ross, W. D., *Aristotle's Prior and Posterior Analytics*, Oxford, 1949.

Runciman, W. G., 'Plato's *Parmenides*', *Harvard Studies in Classical Philology* 64 (1959), 89–120.

Ryle, G., 'Plato's *Parmenides*', *Mind* 48 (1939), 129–51 and 302–25.

Ryle, G., *Plato's Progress*, Cambridge, 1966.

Simplicius, *In Aristotelis Physicorum Libros Quattuor Priores Commentaria*, ed. H. Diels, Berlin, 1882.

Solmsen, F., *Die Entwicklung der aristotelischen Logik und Rhetorik*, in *Neue Philologische Untersuchungen* 4, Berlin, 1929.

Stenzel, J., 'Speusippos', in *Real-Encyclopädie der classischen Altertumswissenschaft* 2 Reihe III 2 (1929), 1636–69.

Stocks, J. L., 'The Composition of Aristotle's Logical Works', *Classical Quarterly* 27 (1933), 115–24.

Strang, C., 'Plato and the Third Man', *Aristotelian Society: Supplementary Volume* 37 (1963), 147–65.

Tricot, J., *Aristote – Organon V – Les Topiques*, Paris, 1965.

Vlastos, G., 'Degrees of Reality in Plato', in *New Essays on Plato and*

Aristotle, ed. J. R. Bambrough, London, 1965.

Vlastos, G., 'The Third Man Argument in the *Parmenides*', *Philosophical Review* 63 (1954), 319–49.

Waitz, T., *Aristotelis Organon* vol. 2, Leipzig, 1846.

Weil, E., 'La Place de la Logique dans la Pensée Aristotélicienne', *Revue de Métaphysique et de Morale* 56 (1951), 283–315.

Wieland, W., 'Das Problem der Prinzipienforschung und die aristotelische Physik', *Kant-Studien* 52 (1960–1), 206–19.

Wilpert, P., 'Aristoteles und die Dialektik', *Kant-Studien* 48 (1956–7), 247–57.

Wisdom, John, *Other Minds*, Oxford, 1952.

Wisdom, John, *Paradox and Discovery*, Oxford, 1965.

Wisdom, John, *Philosophy and Psychoanalysis*, Oxford, 1953.

Wittgenstein, L., *Philosophical Investigations*, ed. G. E. M. Anscombe and R. Rhees, Oxford, 1953.

Wittgenstein, L., *The Blue and Brown Books*, Oxford, 1958.

Zabarella, J., *Opera Logica*, Basle, 1594.

GLOSSARY

The references are to pages where the translations of Greek words are first presented or mainly discussed. For further references to the treatment of the notions thus translated, see also the General index.

adoleschein: chattering, 128
adoxon: implausible, 80
aitia: ground, 18
akribeia: precision, 86
apodeixis: demonstrative science, 10; demonstration, 74
apophasis: negative, 41
aporia: problem, 9
archē: foundation, principle, 23, 31, 117
autos: as such, 99
to boulēton: the object of wish, 55–6
eidos: species, Form, 113
eikos: probability, 78
ek: from, 118
enantios: contrary, 27–8
endoxon: plausible view, 32, 77, 83 (for *endoxos*, see 79)
epagōgē: induction, 20–1
genos: kind, 113
gnōrimon: intelligible (*gnōrimōteron:* more intelligible), 8, 68 (for *gnōrimos*, see 68 n. 28)
haplōs: without qualification, 57, 99
horizesthai: distinguish, 26
kalōs: properly, 110
koinos: common, 40–1
logikos: logical, 29–30, 48
logos: argument, 18; set of words, 105
meros: part, 118
metechein: partake, 113
nous: intuitive reason, 33
orexis: appetite, 94
organon: tool, 33
ousia: substance, reality, 10, 15–16; being, 109
pathos: affection, 109
ta phainomena: the agreed facts, 55
philosophia: philosophy, 12, 34
phusikē: natural philosophy, 131

141

pithanon: persuasive, 76
poion ti: some qualified thing, 109
sophos: savant, 79
sullogismos: reasoning, 20–1
ti ēn einai: essence, 105, 107, 112
ti esti: nature, 10, 108, 112; definition, 28
theologikē: theology, 44
toiosde: such-and-such, 75–6

INDEX OF PASSAGES

ARISTOTLE

GENERAL INDEX

A fortiori arguments, 84
Alexander of Aphrodisias, 1, 81, 112n34, 119
Analytics (see *Topics*)
Anscombe, G. E. M., 58n9, 112n34
Antisthenes, 79, 112n34
Aristotle, method in philosophy, 13, 25, 31–2, 54–5, 56–7 (*see also under separate topics*)
art, contrasted with science, 76–7
attributes, of things in general; discussed in *SE*, 40–1; identified with 'contraries', 28; studied by dialectic and science, 9–12, 13–15, 16, 104; treated in *Topics*, 38–9
Austin, J. L., 65n23, 100n141

Bambrough, J. R., 23, 25n66, 36–7, 53, 59n17
being, complexity of, 11, 42, 43, 45, 47; and dialectic, 14–16, 28–9 (*see also* reality, substance)
Bonitz, H., 10n12
Braun, E., 2, 3
Brunschwig, J., 3

categories, differences of, 46, 50, 108, 131
Charlton, W. E., 15n32
Cherniss, H., 81, 93, 95n118, 96n123, 97n131, 108n18
chronology of Aristotle's works, 1, 4, 37–8, 44n154, 107n18
Chroust, A.-H., 2
compounds, definability of, 107, 118, 129, 131–2
constituents of things, 117–18, 121–2
context-dependence, 101
contraries, and dialectic, 20, 25–9; as things and propositions, 27; in Plato, 100–1 (*see also* attributes)

definition; and dialectic, 19–21, 25,

34–7, 53, 133; and essence, 89, 105, 107–8, 122; consisting of genus and differentia, 108, 109–11, 113–14, 117–20, 122–3; in conjunction form, 114–17, 121–3, 134–5; plurality of its elements, 105–7, 122; proofs of, 107–8n18, 111; proper formation of, 110, 123; subject of, 120–1 122–3, 135; treatment in *Topics* Z–H, 35, 104, 106; uniqueness of, 69–70, 113–14, 118–19, 134; unity of, 120–23, 128, 132, 134 (*see also* compounds, differentia, genus, intelligibility, Plato, realism, *Topics*)
Democritus, 19
demonstration; *ad hominem*, 74; and reality, 10–11, 16–17
de Pater, W. A., 3, 104n5
de Strycker, E., 38n124
dialectic; and human faculties, 70, 75, 91–4, (individuals and groups) 75–7, 83n90; and philosophy, 12–16, 17, 18–19, 29, 31, 34–6, 48–9, 64, 104; and sciences, 5–6, 49–50, 79, 114; as question-and-answer method, 8, 21–2, 25, 32, 52; audience for, 91–2; importance as a method, 2, 29, 31–2, 36–7, 51, 79, 81; study of, 89–94 (*see also* attributes, definition, Forms, induction, intelligibility, logic, *Metaphysics*, Plato, Socrates, sophistic, *Topics*)
differentia; as element in essence and nature, 108–9, 113; in definitions, 109–11, 112, 113; in Plato and Speusippus, 111–12; not predicable of genus, 125–6, 128, 132–3
Diogenes Laertius, 112n34
Dissoi Logoi, 100n142
division, Plato's method of, 111–12, 125–7

92n111, 95, 96n124, 99n137, 101n143, 130; on the *Organon* and other works of Aristotle, 31, 41–3, 48, 64n20

Pacius, J., 1
paradox and common-sense views, 55–6, 79–80, 83–4
Parmenides, first part of, 96–7
Patzig, G., 3, 44n154, 74n50
Peck, A. L., 96n123
peirastic, as part of dialectic, 12, 21n51, 39n134
persuasive, 76, 91
philosophy (*see* dialectic, sciences, universal study)
physics (*see* natural philosophy)
Pickard-Cambridge, W. A., 40n141, 77
Plato; on definitions, 118, 126–7; on dialectic and reality, 7–8, 13, 15–16, 48, 50–2; on knowledge and its objects, 97, 98, 101–2, 122; on relations, 97–8, 100–1 (*see also* division, Forms, foundations, qualified, universality)
plausible views (*endoxa*), 10, 23, 29–30, 32, 38, 79–85, 90, 92; of experts and ordinary people, 79, 80, 82; instances of, 10n12, 29–30, 43, 95, 97 (*see also* qualified)
pleasure, 58, 59
precision; as character of Plato's Forms, 97; in intellectual investigations, 32, 86–7, 88, 89–90
Presocratics, 81
'primary', senses of, 67
principles of things, 117–18
probability, 78
properties, contrasted with definitions, 105, 109
Pythagoreans, 17, 19

qualified/unqualified distinction; in objects of human faculties, 5–6, 59, 85–6, 87–8, 90, 93; in the intelligible, 72–3, 114; in the object of wish, 57–9, 60–1, 62, 63–4, 66–7, 95–6; in the plausible, 80–5; use by Plato, 98–9, 101–3; use in other concepts, 76–7, 81–2, 110n25

Rackham, H., 55n4
realism; extreme form of, 62–4, 67–8, 71–2, 73, 85, 88, 95–6, 100–2;

in theory of definition, 69, 71, 73, 95, 113
reality and appearance, 60, 62, 67, 72, 94–6, 101–2
reasoning, 19, 20–2
relative things, 129–31
relativism, extreme form of, 62–3, 67–8, 71–2, 73, 85, 88, 100
repetition; called 'chattering', 128; in definitions, 123–5, 126–7, 131–3, 134–5; in statements, 127–8, 129–32; vicious and innocent forms of, 124–5, 132
rhetoric, 74, 76–7, 91
Robinson, R., 17nn39–40, 26n69
Ross, W. D., 1, 9, 10–11, 17, 21n49, 25–8, 29, 30n86, 32–3
Runciman, W. G., 26n69, 97n131
Ryle, G., 8n6, 26, 100n142

sciences; special and universal, 5, 39–40, 42, 43–4, 47–9; theory of, in *An. Post.*, 10, 16–17, 22–3 (*see also* attributes, dialectic, foundations)
self-refutation, 81n83
series, 42–4; and definitions, 43
shooting and targets, 57–8, 61
Simplicius, 26n68
Socrates; Aristotle on his dialectic, 19–23, 24–6, 30, 36; on wrong-doing, 30, 55, 88n103
Solmsen, F., 1, 93n113
sophistic (eristic); distinguished from dialectic, 8, 14, 77, 80n76, 91; related to dialectic, 12, 39–40, 75–6, 83–4
sophistical refutations, 39–40
soul, study of, 43, 47n162
Speusippus, 112
Stocks, J. L., 1
Strang, C., 96n124
substance, 9–10, 49–51, 67, 130; and demonstration, 10–11; and reality, 12, 15–17, 28–9
syllogistic, 22n53, 74
synonymity, 119–20, 123, 134

taste, 62–4, 65–6
theology, 42, 44, 67
Topics; and work in Academy, 2, 4; its relation to *Analytics*, 1–3, 89–90, 93–4, 107–8n18; its relation to *Metaphysics*, 37–9, 104, 133–4; on arguments 'in accor-

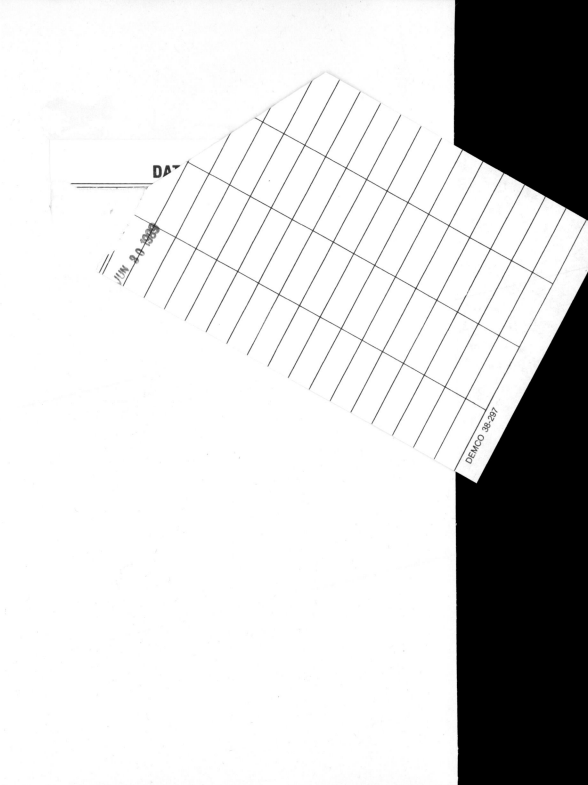

DATE

JUN 30 1989

DEMCO 38-297